ARE WE NORMAL?
FUNNY, TRUE STORIES FROM AN EVERYDAY FAMILY

CHRISTINA SCALISE

GH00469669

BRIGHTON PUBLISHING LLC
435 N. HARRIS DRIVE
MESA, AZ 85203

ARE WE NORMAL?
FUNNY, TRUE STORIES FROM AN EVERYDAY FAMILY

CHRISTINA SCALISE

BRIGHTON PUBLISHING LLC
435 N. HARRIS DRIVE
MESA, AZ 85203
WWW.BRIGHTONPUBLISHING.COM

ISBN13: 978-1-62183-224-9
ISBN 10: 1-621-83224-4

COPYRIGHT © 2014
PRINTED IN THE UNITED STATES OF AMERICA

First Edition

COVER DESIGN: TOM RODRIGUEZ

All rights reserved. No part of this publication may be reproduced or transmitted in any form or by any means, electronic or mechanical, including photocopy, recording, or any information storage retrieval system, without permission in writing from the copyright owner.

ARE WE NORMAL ~ CHRISTINA SCALISE

Sunburn and a Swollen Eye
How Does That Work?
You Should Have Changed the Toilet Paper Roll
Lighting the Smoker
Waxing the Stairs
Ice Hill Sledding
Hot Peppers Are So Good!
Walk the Dogs
Let's Build a Fort
The Hazards of Feeding Chickens
I Broke My A-s-s!
A Concussion and a Broken Foot

ᴄℐᴑACKNOWLEDGEMENTSᴑᴐ

To my husband and children: Thank you so much for helping me remember all the little facts and details within these stories. I truly appreciate your suggestions, opinions, patience, and support in helping me share our stories and sense of humor with the world. I love you all.

To my sisters, mother and my in-laws who also helped with their opinions, suggestions and fact checking; I would also like to express my gratitude. Your help was very much appreciated!

I would also like to thank the staff at Brighton Publishing for once again assisting me in creating the best book possible. Your expert guidance and input always proves to be invaluable.

ᏟᏚᎢNTRODUCTIONᏟᏚᎢ

Let me start by asking a question. Do you consider yourself to be normal? What is normal, anyway? The dictionary defines normal as "the usual, regular, common, typical, average, standard, expected, and ordinary."

These words are definitely not ones I'd use to describe my family. With all the crazy things we've done and have had happen to us over the years, we were often left asking the same question: "Are we normal?"

I originally started writing this book as a journal of stories for my kids to read when they were older and had children of their own—a few funny stories they could tell our future grandchildren about. Then it grew from there, with one story after another. Boy, is our family full of them.

After a while, I figured—why not share our stories with the rest of the world? I'm sure most people can relate to at least one or more of these stories. And if not…well…I hope readers at least get a good laugh out of them.

As with every family, we've dealt with our share of struggles. The way we learned to deal with them was with as much humor as possible. Some days, that was the only thing getting us through it all. Other days—well, what can I say? That's just how we are.

Although these stories have all been approved by the family members involved, I don't mention any of the names of our children. This is simply for their privacy and protection. Regarding some of the stories contained in this book, it also protects their sense of pride.

We're also a family who uses the occasional swear word, so you may see a little of that sprinkled in this book as well. As parents with young children, we tried our best not to swear in front of them. When they were young, we never allowed them to swear. But as they grew older and became young adults, we have relaxed a bit in that area. My intention here isn't to offend anyone with this swearing; I'm only writing about the events as they occurred. So, to those people who think we're all going to hell because we use the occasional swear word, don't worry—we know people there.

I hope readers enjoy this book. If anyone would like to share a story of their own, please visit our website, www.AreWeNormal.com or send an email with the story to AreWeNormal@yahoo.com. While there, sign up for our newsletter to keep updated on future publications.

And remember...life is way too short, so try to enjoy every minute of it with a sense of humor!

CHAPTER ONE

COMMON THINGS HEARD IN OUR HOME

A little side note before we get started here.

The comments related in this chapter were always said in a joking manner and were always taken as such, each and every time. So yes, we love our children…no, we never actually beat them…and no, we never charged them rent. With that being said…enjoy!

Walk into our home on any given day, and one or more of the following phrases may be heard:

"I have three children; do you really think that look is going to work on me?" (This was always said when the kids were giving that pathetic look, hoping for sympathy, and trying to get their way on something.)

"What are you doing?"
"Why would you do that?"
"Don't ever do that again!"

"Are you paying rent?"
"Do you want to start?"

"Are your legs broken?"
"Do your hands still work?"
"Get a job, and then we'll talk."

"Suck it up."
"Suck it up, troop."
"Suck it up, buttercup"
"Oh, just suck it up!"

"When will you be home?"
"Is that guy time or regular time?"

"It was free!"
"It was on sale—and I had a coupon!"

"Did you shower?"
"Did you use soap?"

"Did you brush your teeth?"
"Let me see them."

"Pee goes *in* the toilet!"

"Because I said so, that's why!"

Person One: "You need a hug."
Person Two: "And you need a beating!"

"Blood or fire?"—See Chapter Three

"Bobber!"—See Chapter Eleven

"Do I have *maid* written on my forehead?"

"I'm not doing it for you; you have to learn how to do it yourself."

And a few minutes later…"See, I told you; you could do it. Good job!"

"And what are you going to do for me?"

"I'm officially on strike!"

"If you want something to eat, learn how to cook."

"Finish your dinner, or you'll be eating it for breakfast."

"You know, there are starving children all over the world who'd love to have what you're having right now."

"Come here a minute."

"I'm going to count to three…"
"Last warning!"

"Keep it up—I dare you!"

"This ought to be good; let's see what happens."

"I know where you sleep, and I have bright-red nail polish."

"That's a rookie move."

"Do you want to rephrase that?"

"What's the magic word?"

"Good Lord!"

"Oh sugar!"

"Fudge nuggets!"

"Holy cannoli!"

"Oy vay"

"It's not OCD; it's CDO!"—See Chapter Five

"That's our mother..."

Our children, upon finishing an argument:
Child One: "Your face!"
Child Two: "Your Mom!"
Child One Again: "She's standing right there!"

"Smart ass!"

"I'm not touching youuu."

"He flipped shit!"

"I didn't do it."

"He hit me first!"

"Really?"

Child: "He started it!"
Adult response: "And *I'm* going to finish it!"

"You see, what had happened was…"

"Why did we have children again?"

CHAPTER TWO

LETTERS TO OUR CHILDREN

The high school our two oldest children attended had a special assignment during their senior year. The parents were supposed to write each child a letter of advice for the future.

The first one, written to our son, had to be from one parent, so I wrote that one. The second one, written to our daughter, years later, was from both of us, and was slightly similar to the one I wrote for our son, but had a bit of a gender twist to it.

We still haven't written the one for our other son, as he has yet to reach that particular milestone. I may include that one in a future book.

These letters were both written with a sense of humor intended. And no, I don't truly believe that all men are for decoration only and cannot multi-task...most of the time. *and* yes, my children know that—I think.

According to our daughter, all the other letters that were read aloud in class that day, written by the other parents, included phrases like:

"I'm so proud of you, honey."

"You'll do great things in life."

"We love you so much."

Ours were a bit different:

To our Son,

Here are some motherly/womanly words of advice that you should keep in mind while on your journey through life. I give you these because I love you, and I know you're a man, and will need to be reminded of these things over and over again, so don't throw this away, but instead, read it every morning before you come in contact with any women.

Don't piss off your mother

Don't piss off your girlfriend/wife.

Don't piss off your grandmother.

Don't piss off any woman you'll continue to have contact with.

Always remember—we're women, and we know how to get even.

Always put the toilet seat down—and for the love of God—get the pee in the toilet, not on the outside! No woman appreciates sitting in pee just before falling into a cold bowl of water at 3:00 in the morning.

Never let the gas tank get below a quarter of a tank and then give it to a woman. If we run out of gas, you'll never, ever, ever hear the end of it!

Learn how to do your own banking, and always have enough cash on you.

Don't offer to go shopping with a woman and then disappear at the first sign of hunting equipment.

Pick up your dirty clothes and put them in the hamper. If you live with a woman and notice your dirty clothes have been sitting out for more than two days—it's a test, and you've already failed. Who am I kidding? You're a man—you won't notice. Just be aware that, after two days of not picking up after yourself, you'll be punished! And remember—that rule applies to everything, not just clothes.

Don't ever attempt to do laundry—men are color blind and don't know how to fold. It's just part of your genetics. Either get a maid, or have your girlfriend/wife do it while you attempt to cook her dinner.

When you're in an argument with a woman, always say…"I know, I screwed up, and I'm sorry." It doesn't matter if you think you're right or not. Most often, you won't be, and saying anything else will just prolong your suffering.

Always give hugs and kisses and say "I love you." If not, you'll be seeing some mood swings that you're going to want to blame on PMS—not a good idea.

Don't ever blame anything on PMS. That'll only get you hurt physically.

Now, if you have actually read every word of all of this, then I guess I've done a pretty good job with you. If not, then that was just your male genetics kicking in. You men tend to blank out whenever a woman talks, and you'll probably need to start over again and read the whole thing.

I tell you all of this because I'm your mother and I love you very much, and if I can just keep one toilet seat in the world clean and down, then I can die a happy woman.

Always remember to keep your sense of humor and find the good in everything, and you'll do just fine.

Love always,

Mom

To our Daughter,

Well, you're getting ready for that next big step in life, so here are some words of wisdom that you should keep in mind while on your journey through life.

Don't piss off your mother. I'm always right—and I always win.

Don't piss off any woman you'll continue to have contact with.

Always remember—we're women, and we know how to get even.

Don't take criticism personally; instead, learn to use it to better yourself.

Don't ever become a drama queen, or I'll personally smack the drama right out of you.

Always stand up for what's right, and learn how to stand your ground when needed.

Never let the gas tank get below a quarter of a tank, and always keep $20 in the glove box for emergencies.

Learn how to do your own banking, and always have enough cash on you.

Learn how to be self-sufficient. Men are only for decoration, trust me.

Get organized, and make the extra effort to stay organized! It makes a world of difference in your stress level, happiness, and future.

Men cannot multi-task—don't try to make them—it only confuses them and makes them angry.

When you're in an argument with a man, you'll be right ninety-nine point nine percent of the time, but just remember to throw them a bone once in a while. It makes them feel smart.

Always give hugs and kisses and say, "I love you."

Life is short; live it to the fullest.

I tell you all of this because I'm your mother, and I love you very much.

Always remember to keep your sense of humor, and always try to find the good in everything, and you'll do just fine!

Love always, Mom

From Dad,

Shoot straight and keep your powder dry. Never follow the crowd; always lead the crowd.

Be kind to others, but also be wary of others. Beware of smooth talkers; always look at the total package.

Not everyone you encounter in life will be a nice person.

Never drink from a glass that you didn't prepare.

Stay away from alcohol and drugs—they're both trouble.

Stay smart, and do great things.

Love, Dad

The following words of wisdom are from both of us.

Don't eat yellow snow.

Always keep your sense of humor—and always look at the positive side of life. Your glass should always be half full.

Try to see things from the other person's point of view. Remember, there's always a reason why they do what they do, and there's always a reason for what they say.

Be a good person and be kind to others.

If you have a problem or hit a bump in life, don't give up. Think about the issue and find a way to solve it or move around it.

Never give up on your dreams; anything is possible if you want it badly enough. Just remember—you can do anything, if you set your mind to it.

Take on projects one at a time.

Be a leader—you can lead, follow, or get out of the way. In life, choose to be a leader. Never do something just because the majority of people are doing it. Make your own decisions and stick with them, if you know you're right.

You can always learn from other people, but don't make a decision based on what other people think is right. Always go with your gut instinct. If something is right or wrong, you'll know it.

Study hard in school—knowledge is power. No one can take away your education.

Remember, good things come in time. Don't put yourself in debt because you want everything all at once—it'll come.

Credit cards are a rip-off. Don't overuse credit cards. That'll put you in debt quickly, and you'll waste your hard-earned money in the long run. You may need credit cards to purchase things, but the key is to pay off the bill as soon as possible.

Don't worry about what other people are doing, or what other people have. Everything may not be what it appears to be, so be your own person. If someone can't accept you for what or who you are, then you don't need that person in your life.

Money is a big issue in today's society. Yes, you need money to survive, but that's not everything. Always put some money in the bank. Save as much money as you can, but also remember to live life a little. At the same time, prepare for your future—you never know when an unexpected bill may arise.

Work hard. Don't be lazy. Whatever career you choose, remember to put in an honest day's work. At this point, your career is school, so work hard at it.

College is going to be a wonderful experience. You'll meet new people and learn many things. Just remember, you're there to learn and have fun, but stay focused on earning that degree and doing the best job you're capable of doing.

Material things, such as a fancy new car or whatever, aren't that important. If you can afford a fancy car, good for you; but don't buy things just to impress someone. Again, if someone can't accept you as you are, step away from that person.

There are many things we can share with you. One important thing is that we love you very much and will always be there when and if you need us. You're on the right road to becoming a very successful and good person. In our eyes, you're turning out just fine. Keep up the good work and stay on the right path in life, and always remember, as problems arise, we'll always be there for you.

Love always,

Mom and Dad

CHAPTER THREE

CREATIVE PARENTING

DRINK WATER

As most people already know, drinking water on a regular basis is a crucial part of staying healthy. Teaching this to children and trying to keep them hydrated, however, can become somewhat challenging. We have one particular child who hates to drink water, and sometimes won't even get a drink to go with dinner. Getting them to drink anything (especially water) has always been difficult.

Because of this, every night during dinner, if any of our children didn't have a drink with the meal they were eating, I'd always ask the same question: "Do we have to have a conversation about constipation, and how lack of water and other fluids can cause it?"

It worked every single time.

VELCRO CHILD

As most parents already know, waking up kids for school can be a tremendously frustrating task. You call them and call them, set alarms out of reach, let them know they'll be running late, and yet they still won't budge.

After years of practice, we finally came up with a few good ways to get them to move. First, they'd get a warning or two, and then it was time for the squirt bottle. Yes, we'd actually go in and squirt them with water.

Most of the time, they'd laugh or grunt and hide under the covers, but when this didn't work, I'd move on to a full cup of ice water. (Thankfully, I only had to resort to this once or twice.)

When we didn't want to soak the mattress with a cup of water, we'd try a different approach—flipping their mattress. This usually worked.

Now when I say *usually,* it's because with one particularly stubborn child, this didn't always work. We called this one our Velcro Child. Whenever we'd resort to flipping her mattress, she'd grab hold of it and hang on for dear life.

Even though we'd be experiencing a Velcro Child moment, she generally got up after the mattress was flipped. I guess hanging on for dear life is enough to wake anyone up.

SPRAY-BOTTLE AND FLY-SWATTER DISCIPLINE

Waking up our children wasn't the only thing we used the squirt bottle for. Any time they didn't want to move when told, started arguing with us, or talking back, they'd get a squirt of water as a reminder that they'd better behave, or start moving. This always got their attention.

If the spray bottle didn't work, next was the fly swatter. This was something that came from my mother. It was her weapon of choice when I was growing up, and even though it stung like hell if we caught it just right, we'd all still be laughing as we ran. My kids did the same thing— they laughed and ran, but they always moved, and ninety-nine percent of the time, it worked in accomplishing what I was trying to get them to do—or stop doing, for that matter. All I had to do was walk toward the fly swatter and they'd laugh like crazy and run like hell.

HOW TO SPOT A SCUMBAG

As any good parent knows, protecting children from strangers and anyone who could possibly cause them harm is an absolute must. Teaching them how to identify and stay away from these potentially harmful people, however, can be quite a challenge.

In order to help our children identify and avoid these types of individuals, my husband, in his infinite wisdom, found it necessary to point them out to our kids. He'd often refer to them as scumbags. Although I appreciated what he was trying to do, I wasn't happy about him teaching this word to our children at such a young age.

While walking through the mall one day, our daughter—who was still very young at the time—pointed to a man who was standing close by, acting very inappropriately for his surroundings. She asked, very innocently and yet still quite loudly, "Daddy, is that a scumbag?"

The man turned around and glared at them. He'd obviously heard the question.

My husband then looked back at the man and simply responded by laughing and quickly moving her along as he explained that, when asking that question, it was best to do it quietly.

And yes, by the way—that was a scumbag.

She was so proud she'd actually spotted one all by herself that day, and couldn't wait to tell me all about it when she got home.

As for my husband—well, even after yet another lecture from me, he's still pointing them out to our kids.

Don't Forget to Use Sunblock

Getting children to use sunblock can be quite challenging. In our family, with our fair skin, it's an absolute necessity. After several years and several sunburns on children who didn't want to bother putting it on, I tried a new approach. I'd quickly smear a small amount of sunblock on them in the form of a small line, smiley face, or something else they wouldn't like. If they didn't finish covering that area with sunblock and were burned, they'd have a constant, embarrassing reminder of what would happen if they forgot it again.

Fortunately for them, I was only able to accomplish this a few times, as they quickly learned to watch out for Mom after being told to use the sunblock.

And if they did get sunburn…the standing rule in our home was—and still is—if you forget to use sunblock and get sunburned, you'd better plan on getting smacked from other family members.

This generally added to the incentive to use the sunblock on a somewhat regular basis. Any major sunburns were always treated with extra care, of course, but the average sunburn was always smackworthy.

YOUR UNDERWEAR IS SHOWING

Some kids these days seem to think it's cool to walk around with their pants hanging down and their underwear showing—sometimes as far as their knees. I personally find this so-called fashion statement to be extremely repulsive, and have always taught my kids to keep their underwear from showing at all times.

Although they never purposely showed their underwear, they occasionally had their pants hanging too low and their underwear sticking out when they bent over. Every time I saw this happening, I'd either start out with the old song, "I see London, I see France…" or, if I'd seen their underwear several times that week and they didn't seem to care about it showing anymore, I'd simply yank it up as far as it would go.

For some silly reason, my kids don't bend over in front of me much anymore.

A little side note here: if a child wears his pants like this on purpose, it's often helpful to tell him to look up what it means for someone to let his pants hang that low in prison…They'll usually pull their pants right up to their chest.

MOM HAS EYES IN THE BACK OF HER HEAD?

Children learn at an early age that they can do a lot of things they aren't supposed to be doing when Mom and Dad aren't looking. We dealt with this little problem by telling them that all moms have eyes in the back of their heads and can see everything their kids are doing at all times. This was one of those tricks I'd learned from my mother. When we were driving along in the car and had the benefit of a rearview mirror on hand, they never knew my secret.

One day, while sitting around relaxing at home, my daughter started playing with my hair, moving it all around in different directions. She'd often play with it for a while, trying to fix it into different styles; so I wasn't paying much attention to what she was doing that day.

Then I realized her hairstyling job was taking a lot longer than usual, so I asked what she was trying to do. She said she was looking for my extra set of eyes that were supposed to be in there somewhere. She couldn't understand why she couldn't find them.

MOM CAN SEE THROUGH THE TABLE?

Most families that have two or more children have had them, at one point or another, start kicking each other underneath the table. They always think that if Mom can't see it or hear it, she doesn't know what's going on. Growing up with three sisters, I was usually one of those children doing the kicking. My mother curbed this little problem by telling us she could see through the table.

As my children started doing the same thing, I let them know about mothers with X-ray vision, and how any woman could see through the table once they became a mother. I also let them know that if they continued to kick each other, they'd lose their chairs and have to finish eating their dinner while standing at the table instead of sitting. This worked great—I only had to confiscate their chairs a few times. But after a while, they started kicking each other after dinner in other areas of our home. Apparently, they didn't realize that moms can see through more than just kitchen tables.

THERE ARE STARVING CHILDREN ALL OVER THE WORLD

Whenever a child in our home was refusing to finish dinner, they'd often hear things like, "Finish your dinner, or no snack," or "Finish your dinner, or you'll be eating it for breakfast," or the classic, "You know, there are starving children all over the world who'd love to have what you're having right now." Typically, one of these statements would work in motivating our children to finish their meal.

Unfortunately, these words came back to haunt me one afternoon, as I didn't want to finish my dinner. My son came over to me and repeated the words I'd said to him over and over for years: "You know, Mom, there are starving children all over the world who'd love to have what you're having right now."

I looked over at this child, who was now grinning from ear-to-ear, knowing he'd just used my own words against me, and simply said with a smile; "Then go ahead and mail it to them, because I'm done." Completely dumbfounded, he responded, "All those years I had to finish my dinner. Why didn't I think of that?"

Ha! Mom always wins.

BLOOD OR FIRE?

For sanity's sake, we had a standing rule in our home that, after a certain time at night, our children weren't allowed to bother me or their father for anything other than emergencies.

This also became a rule if we were trying to concentrate while working on a specific project or talking on the phone. I'd always tell them that if the problem didn't involve someone bleeding, or something on fire, they'd better not bother us during that time. If they did bother us, as soon as they'd start talking, they'd always get interrupted with, "Ah, ah, ah...hold on...blood or fire? Neither? Then why are you bothering me?"

Once they heard that question, they usually gave an exhausted look of frustration and walked away, or they ran like hell, depending on the look I was giving them at the time.

Best rule ever!

POTTY TRAINING

Teaching children how to use the potty isn't always easy. It's a very scary concept for a young child, so the parent has to use a lot of excitement and positive reinforcement to be successful.

For our boys, we'd try to give them something to aim at. The most common item we used were small pieces of cereal thrown into the toilet bowl. They'd float around on top of the water. The boys would take aim and try to hit the pieces of cereal. I don't remember how we came up with that idea, but it worked—that is, until we said, "Wow, great job!"

Then they'd turn their entire body around to look at us, while still peeing!

Lesson learned: Wait until they're finished peeing, then give positive reinforcement. Doing this can save a lot of paper towels.

CREATIVE CAMPING TOILETS

Anyone who has ever had the experience of camping with children who have never used the outdoors as their personal toilet before knows how much work it can be to convince a child that it is indeed okay to go outside to pee while camping.

Convincing them there are no toilets available to sit on is a whole other issue. We've had our share of challenges in this area.

One child protested and held it in until we built them a makeshift toilet seat using rocks we'd found around the campsite. Another one needed sheets hung in the trees for privacy. Yet another one used a hollowed-out tree to sit on, and then proudly proclaimed to their other siblings later that day, "I pooped in a tree!"

We haven't camped out in years—any guesses why?

CHAPTER FOUR

THOSE CUTE AND CRAZY KIDS!

SO BLESSED

We've always taught our children to be as independent as possible. Over the years, we've seen them showing their independence in many different ways.

One day, our daughter—around three years old at the time—was busy playing with her toys when she suddenly sneezed. Everyone else in the house was busy doing their own thing at that time, and no one had noticed the sneeze. She looked around and saw there were other people in the house within earshot, and yet no one had said anything. *Why not?* she wondered. *Weren't they paying attention? Aren't we supposed to say "God bless you" anytime someone sneezed? What would happen if I wasn't blessed?*

Not knowing quite what to do, she simply shrugged her shoulders and said, "God bless me." Then she went back to playing with her toys. Incredible...age three, and she already knew how to bless herself. Talk about advanced. What an independent child.

SLEEPING BABIES

There's nothing more precious than a sleeping newborn; and after having three children who rarely took naps, we learned to appreciate those moments when they finally did fall asleep.

One child in particular never took a nap unless he was extremely ill—that is, until he hit his teenage years. Then we had a whole different kind of sleeping issue to deal with.

One day, when this same child was around six weeks old, I placed him down in his bassinet for a quick nap. He looked so precious and content as he slept—how cute! What a rare moment in time that was.

As I stared at my sleeping child, enjoying the quiet moment we were having; I leaned down and gave him a quick kiss on the cheek. In response, he started to wriggle around a bit. Apparently, I'd disturbed him. As he adjusted his sleeping position, he felt the need to give me the finger while continuing to sleep. So much for trying to have a sweet little moment.

Oh well, he was still precious and cute—and more importantly, he was still asleep, thank God!

BABY POWDER IS AWESOME!

To a young child, baby powder can be an extremely fascinating product. You can even make your own clouds with it—yes, clouds.

Our son learned that little trick when he found a bottle of baby powder one day and proceeded to shake it all over his bedroom.

It was one of those days when I was trying to get a few things done around the house while the kids were busy playing in their rooms. Suddenly, I noticed it was just too quiet. I hadn't heard anything from our child's bedroom in a while. As I headed up the stairs to check on him, I knew it wasn't going to be good.

Just as I opened the bedroom door, I was able to see the last of the baby powder being sprayed into the air. It was everywhere!

The whole room was white, including our son, who was now looking at me with a smile on his face. That smile suddenly turned to a look of concern when he saw the look of astonishment on my face.

Not only had this child completely covered the room in baby powder, but he'd also found a jar of Vaseline, and managed to smear his entire body—from head to toe—with it before dispensing the baby powder. He was absolutely covered!

He was so lucky he was still young and cute at that time. What a horribly sticky and messy combination. That took an entire day to clean up.

Before that day, I didn't know that baby powder couldn't be vacuumed up. It just comes out the other end of the vacuum, in what looks like a puff of smoke...and makes your husband laugh like crazy.

BEST HIDING PLACE EVER!

Do you have a child who loves to climb? We have one who climbed on just about everything. Over the years, he even learned how to crawl up the walls in the hallway of our home. He'd brace himself against each opposing wall, with one foot and one hand on each wall, and then slowly crawl up toward the ceiling, one step at a time. Once he reached the ceiling, he'd then hang in place until his arms got tired.

While playing a game of hide-and-seek one afternoon, he decided to use this little skill to his advantage. He crawled up the walls of the hallway and hid in plain sight near the ceiling, where he was sure he wouldn't be noticed. I didn't think that was a great idea. First of all, I wasn't happy he'd learned how to crawl up the wall leaving handprints and footprints along the way each time. Second, I didn't think he'd remain undiscovered in plain sight like that. But I decided to stay quiet and let him try it anyway.

His sister, who was playing with him at the time, finished counting to ten and then started her search. In doing so, she walked directly underneath him. He was now grinning from ear-to-ear, trying not to laugh, and struggling like crazy to stay in place. I couldn't believe it! How could she not notice someone who was in plain sight, hanging directly above her like that?

About a minute or so later, hanging in place was no longer an option. His arms and legs began to get tired, and they started to weaken. He dropped down to the floor and was suddenly in view.

Hearing the loud thump, our daughter ran over to him. She was completely astonished that her brother had just appeared out of nowhere. It was magic! How did he do that? She was simply amazed. And he was so proud; his little trick had worked.

Best hiding place ever!

HALLOWEEN HAYRIDE

One Halloween, my children and I went on a haunted Halloween hayride with my sisters and all their kids. Everyone was excited to go. On the way there, they were all talking about how scary they thought the hayride would be, and how much fun they were going to have.

When we arrived, the kids were the first ones out of the vehicles. Without hesitation, they ran to get in line for the hayride. They all had smiles on their faces and were checking out every Halloween decoration along the way. They couldn't wait—the anticipation was almost too much.

The hay wagon finally pulled up, and the kids piled on. We were all sitting together on bales of hay, waiting for the ride to start. As we waited, they were getting more and more excited. It was starting to get dark outside and the scary setups that were on display were now lighted up and waiting for them, just ahead.

As they were looking around at the displays, I noticed my daughter (about four years old at the time) was no longer looking excited. I started to watch her facial expressions as we drove up to the first stop on the hayride. She was now looking very nervous. *Oh, this is not going to be good,* I thought.

As the first scary actor made his way around the wagon, trying to grab and scare the children as he went, I felt her grab me. Then I heard her start to scream and cry.

I hugged her tight and told her there was nothing to worry about. I assured her that the man was just an actor, trying to scare us for some Halloween fun. She wasn't buying my story.

The hayride then continued on to the next stop, where I saw another actor heading toward the wagon with a chainsaw in his hand. Yup, it was definitely a chainsaw! *Oh boy,* I thought. *This isn't going to help calm her down at all!*

As he approached the wagon with his chainsaw running as loud as he could get it to go, my daughter started screaming bloody murder. She proceeded to crawl up underneath my shirt to hang on for dear life. Well, guess

31

what? I already had a child in there. I was about eight months pregnant at the time, and there wasn't any space left in my shirt for her to go.

I'm not sure how she did it, but somehow she still managed to find enough room to squeeze in. At that point, everyone riding on the hay wagon with us was now laughing hysterically at my situation. My shirt was now up to its very limits and I looked totally absurd.

This, unfortunately, was where my daughter remained until the hayride was over. Needless to say, that was her very last haunted hayride ever.

I'M GONNA GET ICE CREAM!

After more than twenty-three years of raising children, my husband and I took our first vacation ever without them. I know…ridiculous, right? I don't know why it took us so long. We only spent two days away, but it was really fun and relaxing to be kid-free for a while.

At home, all three kids were also enjoying their newfound freedom in a parent-free environment. We'd told them before we left that they should all go out to dinner together without us. They were all getting old enough so we thought it would be a good idea. Two of them were teenagers and one was already in his early twenties.

They thought dinner out sounded great; so one night our two boys drove together to pick up their sister after work at a local animal hospital. They all went out to a nearby restaurant together.

During dinner, our daughter decided to describe in detail what she'd learned to do at work that day. Unfortunately, the procedure she was describing was something most people would find absolutely revolting. She thought it would be funny to give very specific details as she explained it.

Of course, our sons didn't appreciate hearing all those little details while they were eating their meal, and they didn't think the other restaurant patrons who were within earshot appreciated it very much, either. But even though they were a little grossed out and embarrassed, they were all still laughing the entire time.

After dinner, they decided to go out for ice cream. As they walked up the parking lot toward the ice cream place, our semi-adult daughter, still in her obnoxious green scrubs from work, thought it would be funny to continue embarrassing both brothers.

She tried to grab both of them by the arms as she started skipping through the parking lot, singing very loudly, "I'm gonna get ice cream! I'm gonna get ice cream!"

By this time, everyone in the parking lot was now staring at them. Consequently, our daughter was then shoved ahead by both brothers, still singing and skipping along as they walked into the ice cream shop.

Yup, that's our teenage and adult kids unsupervised. They actually went out for dinner and ice cream...together...without us...and managed to put on a fabulous show for everyone around them. Who wouldn't be proud?

Chapter Five

PARENTS ARE A LITTLE CRAZY, TOO!

CONCERT TIME

Ah, rock concerts...such a wonderful part of a teenager's life, and a somewhat stressful part of a parent's life.

As a young teenager, our son and his friend both enjoyed heavy metal music very much. So when their favorite band had an upcoming concert planned a few hours from our home, they decided they wanted to attend and asked for permission to go.

This sort of concert was what most people would classify as the head-banging type. Knowing how some of those could be, my husband and I weren't too thrilled about them going alone together. We told them they'd only be allowed to go if he went with them.

Both kids agreed, and the tickets were then purchased.

The day finally arrived, and the boys were both very excited. They couldn't wait to go. On the long drive to the concert, late that afternoon, my husband gave his usual speech about how they should be safe and watch out for certain types of people and avoid certain situations.

They agreed to be careful, and then started laughing and teasing him about how much he was going to stand out in the crowd. Apparently, middle-aged men don't blend in very well at these types of concerts.

As they arrived and started walking down the street toward the building, they noticed that the crowd gathering outside looked like the usual heavy metal, head-banging type, with the exception of the church group who was adamantly protesting the concert at that time. My husband didn't like the looks of some of those in attendance, or the rough-looking neighborhood they were in. He told both kids to stay close to him.

As they approached the front entrance, they noticed a police officer standing there, watching each person walk through the doors. He was glad to see there was some form of security at the concert, and started to walk through the doors behind the kids.

As he walked in, the policeman asked him to stop. He wanted to search him. My husband couldn't believe it. Had this man seen the crowd of people walking in? He was the only normal-looking person in attendance. With the way some of the people in that crowd looked, acted, and—quite frankly—smelled of illegal substances, why in the world would the officer have chosen to search him? He couldn't believe it, but fully cooperated as both kids watched in amusement, laughing hysterically as he was thoroughly searched. Bunch of smart asses!

After the search was over, they all continued inside so the boys could enjoy their concert. As for my husband— well, after being thoroughly searched in front of two hysterical teenagers and then suffering through a head-banging concert that seemed to last forever…well…needless to say, that was the last head-banging concert he ever attended.

OMG! Another Concert

A couple of years later, our daughter, a young teenager at the time, wanted to attend a concert with her friend. And once more, my husband volunteered to go with them.

I was so thrilled; I don't know how I managed to get out of going to this one, too, but I promised him I'd definitely get the next one—which I did.

They were soon on their way.

As they arrived at the concert, they noticed a long line of very excited teenagers starting to form at the entrance of the building outside. It was a nice, somewhat normal concert—no head-banging crowd to deal with this time.

There were a few other parents who'd arrived with their kids, as well. It was one of those concerts a parent just had to attend for the child's sake, but couldn't wait for it to be over. Knowing this ahead of time and trying to keep himself amused while in attendance, my husband had decided it would be fun to tease and embarrass our child as much as possible that day.

As they drove past the entrance, he noticed two young men happily skipping along together, holding hands. He immediately started to laugh as he pointed them out to the kids. The men were obviously very excited to be at the concert.

Knowing that the window was down all the way and others standing on the sidewalk right next to them had probably just heard him pointing out the men and laughing, our daughter was now thoroughly embarrassed. She slumped down into the back seat of our car as her friend burst into laughter. He thought he was being funny, but she was not amused! He then dropped off the kids so they could hold their place in line while he parked the car.

As he walked up to the entrance to find them standing in line, he noticed the excitement was building more and more within the crowd. He just couldn't help himself. As he reached the kids, he immediately started to jump up and down with a huge smile of excitement, saying, "Oh my God! We're going to see...!" They couldn't believe what he'd just done.

"Oh my God" was right. He was a grown man, jumping up and down like a crazed teenage girl, in front of a huge crowd of strangers. And those strangers now all knew he was with them!

Our daughter was mortified; but the other parents standing in line—and the friend who was with them at the time—all found it hysterical.

It was at this point that I started receiving text messages from our daughter, saying how embarrassing her father was acting, what he'd done, and how she was never going to attend another concert with him ever again.

I took a couple of minutes to gather myself together after laughing my butt off. Then I took some time to send a text message to my husband, telling him to behave and stop embarrassing the kids.

After the concert had started and the kids were busy enjoying themselves, he then stood off into the background, still within eyesight, and took some time to relax. *Oh, how one nice, cold beer would taste,* he decided. He walked over to the refreshment stand and placed his order, only to find out that that specific concert didn't allow the sale of alcohol.

That was it; he'd had it. He couldn't tease the kids anymore, he was stuck at this boring concert, and he couldn't get one, lousy beer? This concert sucked!

At this point I received a text message from him saying I was definitely going to the next one. I started to laugh as I thought to myself, *Really? That's where the line in the sand is drawn? Really?*

Don't worry, I texted back. *I'll put a beer in the fridge for you for when you get home.*

APPLE LOLLIPOPS

As any good hunter knows, camouflage, lack of scent, and a quiet environment are all very important parts of hunting. My husband knows this, and is always careful to incorporate all of these little details into every hunting trip he goes on.

Being a supportive wife, I occasionally like to go with him when he hunts, to keep him company. He usually enjoys this, except for those days when I decide to bring a snack or two with me.

After sitting in the tree stand with him one morning for what seemed like hours, waiting for a deer to come along, I started to get a little hungry and decided to unwrap a lollipop so I could have a quick snack.

As I started doing this, my husband looked at me with a quizzical look of both confusion and agitation. Then he asked me how I thought eating a lollipop was going to help him get a deer.

I thought about it for a minute, and then explained with a smile, "Well, deer like apples, and the lollipop is apple flavor, so the apple smell from the lollipop should attract the deer."

I was kidding, of course, but he didn't find it funny at all.

Needless to say, he didn't appreciate the real apple I brought with me the following hunting trip, either.

A NORMAL MOM

I just happen to be one of those people who can appreciate almost any type of music. For me, it all depends on the song itself. But my absolute favorite music of all time is hard rock and heavy metal. According to my children, this is *not* the type of music a normal mom would listen to.

Does this really mean I'm not a normal mom, just because I happen to enjoy that type of music? My children think so, and constantly tease me, saying I must be the devil in disguise, because "No normal mom listens to that kind of music!"

Personally, I disagree. I've met plenty of other normal moms who like that kind of music as well, so I'm not the only one!

My kids and I actually like some of the same music; so we play it in the car together often. They just love to get in the car with their friends when I'm driving and say, "Wait...listen for the music that's about to play. It's her music." Then, as hard rock music begins to pump through the car at a fairly high volume, their friends develop shocked looks on their faces. Apparently, I don't look like the hard-rock type.

Of course, my kid's response every time is, "Yup, that's my mom—she's the devil." Real nice!

IT's NOT OCD, IT's CDO!

I've been organizing things my entire life. When my children were young, I'd spend time organizing each room in our home until they all functioned at their absolute best.

I've also helped friends and family organize their homes, worked as a professional organizer, maintain a website called OrganizeYourLifeAndMore.com, and have also written two other books all about organizing. So, as one can imagine, organizing is clearly a huge part of my life. Naturally, it's easy to imagine what the inside of my home looks like, right? Or is it?

In a perfect world, I'd have my home kept clean, neat, and well-organized 24-7, but as we all know, we do not live in a perfect world.

Along with my daily attempt at keeping my home clean and well-organized, I also like to position a few things so they're facing a certain way. It's not really an obsession…more like a strong preference.

My family members understand this. They make fun of me and tease the heck out of me for it...but they do understand it.

Of course, mixing my strong preference for facing things a certain way with a family full of not-so-organized smart asses can make for a pretty difficult and sometimes humorous day.

One day, while I was reorganizing the spice cabinet for what seemed the tenth time that year, I started placing each container the right way—into alphabetical order, with all the labels facing forward so they'd be easy to find.

My husband started to laugh as he stood there watching what I was doing. Then said to me, "You don't have OCD; you have CDO!"

I asked him, "Okay, I know what OCD is, and I know I don't have that; but what the heck is CDO?"

He explained it to me, "It's like OCD (Obsessive Compulsive Disorder) but all the letters are in alphabetical order—like they should be."

Okay, I had to agree with that one—the letters really do need to be in order!

MESSING WITH MOM

Oh, how my family loves to mess with me and my CDO-type tendencies. Any time I'd have something placed a

43

certain way, I could almost guarantee that one of them was going to come along and mess it up, just to drive me insane.

To give a few examples of what I'm talking about...

Toilet paper rolls: Lots of people have a preference on how they want the toilet paper to be dispensed in their home. I'm not the only one, honest.

In our home, the toilet paper rolls are supposed to go in the over position—the right way. That's the rule...never under; always over. That is, until the children decide to be little smart alecks and place them in the upside-down position on purpose, waiting to see how long it'll take me to discover what they've done, and then, of course, fix it.

God knows I can't leave it like that. It has to go in the over position or I wouldn't be able to sleep!

The Chicken Dish: Many people have grown up with a favorite candy dish that they remember using as a small child. My mother had one in the shape of a chicken that I absolutely adored, so when I found a similar one in an antique store, I purchased it right away.

At home, I found the perfect spot for it in the corner of a windowsill, where the sun wouldn't hit it and melt any candies inside. I cleaned it up, filled it with candies, and positioned it just right, so it was facing in, toward the middle of the windowsill. It looked perfect.

Soon after that day, my family—all three kids and my husband—all thought it would be funny to turn the chicken dish around so it was facing the opposite way, just to see if I'd notice.

Of course, I did. I noticed it as soon as I walked into the room. Without hesitating, I turned it back around, so it was facing the right way. I didn't say anything to anyone, because—silly me—I assumed that one of the kids had grabbed a piece of candy out of it and, without paying attention, had accidentally replaced the cover the wrong way. Why would I have thought anything else? No one was laughing or even looking in my direction...or so I'd thought, anyway.

I then walked back out of the room to continue what I'd been working on earlier. As soon as I walked away, they decided it would be even funnier to keep this little form of torture going as long as possible. They turned it back around once again.

When I came back into the room the second time and saw that it had been turned around again, I knew I was being messed with. I fixed it once more, so it was facing the right way, and then turned my attention to the group of hysterical goofballs standing in the room with me, laughing their rear ends off and threatened to beat the next person who dared to touch it again.

Of course, this now became a challenge—to see whether they could continue turning it around without getting caught. This was years ago, and still goes on in our home.

I need a new dish; maybe a plain, old round one this time.

The Pull String Christmas Bear: It doesn't end with the toilet paper roll or the chicken dish. We also have a stuffed, musical Christmas bear that hangs on one specific doorknob every holiday season.

When they were little, the kids would love to pull the string on this bear to hear the music play. Over the years, it simply became a tradition to hang it there.

Unfortunately for me, this has also become a great source for teasing Mom.

I always hung this stuffed bear on the doorknob so it was facing away from the door, so we could see its face—the right way!

The children find it funny, however, to turn it around facing the door, so we see the back of its head instead. Now, whenever I'm not paying attention, it gets turned around. Then I always yell, "Who did it this time?" They all laugh in response and run like the wind.

Believe it or not, I still have yet to catch the person or persons doing this. My theory is—they *all* do it.

The Pantry: Ah, my beautiful pantry. With all the small apartments and homes we've lived in over the years, having a large pantry had always been a dream of mine. When it finally came time to build our new home, I made sure it was included in our plans.

Once our home was built, it was the first area of our home I utilized. I filled it with supplies, arranged all the items inside in the most organized fashion I could possibly manage, and by the time I was done, it looked beautiful. It was the kind of pantry you would see in an organizing magazine.

And, when the toilet paper is in the correct position, my chicken dish is no longer out, and the Christmas bear is put away for the season, my family will then start messing with my beautiful pantry. They turn cans, boxes, and packages upside down and backward, and then stack them in funny ways, just to agitate me.

The best thing about that pantry, though, is that it has a door on it. If I can manage to catch the person in the act of messing it up, I can shut the door and lock them in until they fix what they did.

Ha! I love my new pantry.

CHAPTER SIX

MONEY DOESN'T GROW ON TREES

REST STOP RIP-OFF

While out on a road trip one day, our family decided it was time to take a short break at a rest stop to stretch our legs and refuel the car. Ordinarily, this kind of stop would take a few minutes or so and then we'd be on our way. But not on this particular day.

We pulled up to the gas pump. My husband got out of the car and, since he still refused to pay using anything other than cash at the time—not the case anymore, thank God—he had to go inside to pay the cashier before he could start refilling the tank.

He told the cashier to give him a certain amount in gas, paid for it, and walked back outside toward the car. As he was pumping the gas, the pump unexpectedly shut off before it reached the amount he'd paid for.

He played with the nozzle for a minute or so, trying to get the last of the gas to go into the tank, but it wouldn't turn back on. Not knowing what else to do, he replaced the nozzle, screwed the gas cap back on, got back into the car, and drove over to a nearby parking spot so he was out of the way for the next customer.

As he was driving over to park the car, he started mumbling under his breath a bit and then abruptly announced, to no one in particular, "They just ripped me off!"

Now, thinking the amount of gas he was cheated out of was a substantial amount, I asked him how much the difference was. As he got out of the car and started to walk away, I thought I heard him mutter something about ten cents in response to my question, but wasn't quite sure whether I'd heard him correctly.

As the kids and I sat there, watching him walk back in to talk with the gas station attendant, I turned around and asked if anyone had heard what their father had just said.

Based on the blank looks I was getting, I quickly determined that I wasn't the only one who was confused by his mumbled answer.

"Did he say he was going back in for ten cents?" I asked. "No, he couldn't possibly be going back in for only a dime. It must be a few dollars and ten cents."

So we waited.

A few minutes later, he returned to the car, still looking a bit frustrated, but also a little more satisfied. He'd obviously gotten his money back. He then got back into the car. As we started driving away, I asked him how much money he'd received.

He then looked at me and proudly stated, "Ten cents!"

At that point, we all had trouble controlling our laughter.

Amidst the ongoing fits of continuous chuckling, he then went on to explain how ridiculous it was not to receive what you'd already paid for. Then he went on his usual rant about corporate rip-offs and how the kids should never let any company get away with cheating them out of their money.

Yup, that's my husband—it's not the amount of money, it's the principle, damn it!

THE TEN-YEAR PLAN FOR VEHICLES

In an effort to save money over the years, each new—or semi-new—vehicle we've ever owned has had to last us ten years or more. At least, that's always been the plan, according to my husband. And this plan, for the most part, was acceptable to me, since most of our vehicles were either brand new or almost new when we first purchased them.

However, with that being said, a few of them should have been given up well before the ten-year mark. Convincing him of this, however, was, and still is, extremely hard to do. You see, he likes to get his money's worth out of everything.

The first new vehicle we ever owned was a small economy car that ran great for many years, but after about nine years or so of using it daily, it was starting to fall apart.

Now, when I say "falling apart," I mean there was a small hole starting to develop through the rust in the floor, we had to hold or tie the driver's side door closed to keep it shut, and it occasionally needed a push start…yes, an actual push start.

It took a lot of convincing, but once we hit the ten-year mark, my husband didn't have much choice. With all the problems that had started to surface, we had to get rid of the car. Yay! That one was finally gone.

The next vehicle we purchased was a brand-new minivan. It was great for carting around the kids and all their stuff when they were younger, but it also just barely made it to the ten-year mark. Toward the end, rust was starting to appear everywhere, and the engine was starting to fail. He didn't protest too badly when we decided to get rid of that one, since he knew the engine would have been extremely costly to replace. We ended up donating that one to a local charity—good for them and us.

Next was an SUV. This one was about a year old when we purchased it. It had a superb engine that would start up every time, no matter how cold it was outside, it could tow almost anything we hooked up to it, and it had plenty of room inside for the entire family to fit comfortably.

It was my absolute favorite vehicle to drive when we first bought it, but after eight or nine years of driving it daily, rust spots were starting to form, and the body itself was starting to fall apart. I told my husband it was time to consider replacing it, but of course, we hadn't hit the ten-year mark with it yet, so he refused.

By the time we did reach the ten-year mark, we were having more than just a few rust problems with it. The rear window wiper had stopped working, the back door had to be opened and closed using a bungee cord because the latch had broken so many times it was now beyond repair, and after slamming it shut so many times, it also had a huge dent in it. To top it all off, the blower for the air had also stopped working, making the window defrost feature downright useless.

After being forced to drive this atrocious-looking vehicle a few times in that horrible condition, I'd had it. I told my husband his ten years had been up for a while now, the repairs were starting to cost us too much money, and I was officially done driving it. That was it; it had to go.

He, however, didn't agree. He argued that the engine was still running strong, and he didn't want to spend money on another new vehicle. After a little bit of negotiating, we finally came to an agreement: the next time we had a repair that was over $100, it would be time to replace it.

This now became a challenge for him. It was no longer about saving money; now it was about how long he could keep it running and drive me insane. Every time we had another problem, he'd somehow find a way to get it fixed either for a very low cost, or even for free. His friends, coworkers, and even our next-door neighbor would help him out. I don't know how he kept doing it. Hundred-dollar repairs would somehow be accomplished for only a few dollars, or even a simple case of beer.

One afternoon, he came home from work and noticed a flat tire. He and the kids were all convinced that I'd slashed it. "Mom hates that thing!" one of the kids announced.

Of course, I hadn't touched the tire; but by then, everyone knew I hated the vehicle and wanted it gone. Now sabotage was always on their minds whenever there was a problem with it.

Once the muffler went for the second time, I refused to drive it. I told my husband he could no longer use our other vehicle and stick me with our SUV for any reason at all. I could deal with all the other little problems, and could even take the embarrassment of riding around in a rusted-out vehicle once in a while, but I absolutely refused to announce that I was on the way as I drove it with an extra-loud muffler.

To top it all off, now the driver's side door was failing to open—only for me, of course. He refused to get it fixed. He couldn't understand why it was so difficult for me to "just screw the bolts of the door back in" so I could get back out.

"It's easy," he explained.

Ugh! Really? I thought. *He can't be serious! No one should have to screw the door of their vehicle back together before getting into it, just so they can get back out of it each and every time!*

He then decided that if he could somehow manage to get the muffler fixed for a low cost, it would be worth it to keep the vehicle a little bit longer. When winter was over, we'd once again talk about getting a new vehicle to replace it.

I agreed to this only because I knew that installing a new muffler would cost more than $100, and since we'd agreed that that was our spending limit, he'd have no choice but to replace it.

He then proceeded to search for the receipt from the first muffler we'd purchased, a couple of years prior, and for the first time ever, he actually found it.

Damn it! I thought. *I knew he knew how to use my filing system! I'll bet he knows how to separate colors for the laundry, too!*

He then called the shop where he'd purchased the muffler, and had it replaced for $30. They only charged him for labor, because the warranty was still good. He came back home smiling, knowing he'd just won another battle for his favorite vehicle. Ugh. That thing had to go.

A few more months went by. Our other vehicle, a car that we'd purchased a few years earlier, had been giving us more and more problems. We'd only had it for about five years, but it seemed like each week we were dealing with a new problem. At that point, he and I both knew it would never make it to the ten-year mark.

As we were out car shopping one day, hoping to eventually replace our obnoxious-looking SUV, we came across a nice, new vehicle at a great price. It was a deal my husband just couldn't ignore. Since we both liked it, I knew it was going to be my best chance to finally convince him to purchase a new vehicle and replace our old one. I couldn't wait—we were finally going to replace that ... SUV!

Unfortunately, as we'd driven around in our car that day, I started to notice some problems. Each time I hit the lock button, it would no longer make the normal beeping sound in response, but instead made more of a pathetic half-beep kind of noise. It sounded pitiful, and I swear it was trying to tell us it was dying.

It had also been jumping forward every time we stopped and then started to go again. This had been an ongoing problem that we thought we'd fixed, but it was obviously back once again.

As my husband and I stood there, discussing whether to purchase the new vehicle in front of us, we suddenly found ourselves talking about replacing the car instead of the SUV I'd hated so much, for so long.

I couldn't understand how it had come to this! We'd just discussed selling the SUV the week before, and had it all planned out. I was so close! But unfortunately, our car was now starting to cost more in repairs than the SUV was, and after the day we'd just had with it, I knew it wasn't going to last much longer.

I reluctantly agreed to trade in the car instead, but only after he agreed to replace the SUV the following year, after one more winter with it.

Ugh! I couldn't believe I had to give up my five-year-old car instead of our ten-year-old SUV. How did it ever come to that?

After we'd made the final decision to trade in the car, we talked with the salesman and started filling out the paperwork for our new vehicle. It was one of those deals where we'd driven in with our old car, and a few hours later, were driving out in a new vehicle.

We couldn't believe how quickly we'd just replaced our car, after all those months of researching, test-driving, and negotiating. Dealerships move so fast these days! Way too fast for my husband—he looked like a deer caught in the headlights when the salesman told us we'd be leaving with a new vehicle in less than an hour. He wasn't going to be able to go home and do more research and obsess about what we'd just purchased, to find out whether we'd overpaid before we picked up our new vehicle. How would he ever be able to live with that?

All I could think of at that point was, *Thank God!* I couldn't take much more of the car shopping, researching, and negotiating process with him. We'd been doing that little dance for way too long already.

Right after the last paper was signed, the salesman walked away to process our paperwork. As I looked over at my husband, he had a mischievous grin starting to appear on his face.

I couldn't figure out why he was smiling, so I asked him, "What? Why are you smiling like that?"

And he simply responded , "I win."

That was it; that was all he said.

I could feel my jaw drop open. He'd done it again, and was absolutely loving it! He'd somehow managed to keep his SUV for yet another winter. That smug little ass!

That was back in October of 2012.

Oh, and did I mention we still have the damn thing…and…it's still running? Ugh. Maybe this spring we'll replace it.

CHAPTER SEVEN

DON'T TELL YOUR MOTHER

This segment is dedicated to our beloved Pop, also known to our children as "Poppy"—their great-grandfather. This was my husband's grandfather, who passed away in June of 2012 at the age of 92. He was a remarkable man who loved his family, and most of all, his grandchildren and great-grandchildren. He spent as much time with them as he could, had the best stories, a wonderful sense of humor, and is truly missed by us all.

I remember him telling stories of my husband when he was young, and all the wonderful advice he'd give us about raising our kids. The one piece of advice that stood out to me the most was when he compared children to growing trees. He explained to me, "If you don't keep them straightened out now, when they're young, you'll never be able to fully straighten them out later, when they're older." That is so true.

Our children remember Poppy giving them advice about life, education, dealing with us parents—not always appreciated, but usually funny as hell—and also warning them about staying out of trouble. They also remember him saying things like, "Honey, I'm always in trouble; I've been in trouble my whole life."

My husband, who absolutely adored his grandfather, remembers all the fun times he spent with him as a young child. As a result of a lot of those fun times they had together, he remembers Poppy saying a different phrase: "Don't tell your mother."

Playing Poker with the Guys

As my husband tells it, Pop was the best grandfather a kid could ever have. He took him and his cousins everywhere, and even let them play poker with the men at the cattle sales they went to. They'd be sitting around with these men who were playing cards, smoking cigars, and snacking on the food that was all around them, feeling more grown-up than ever.

When they'd lose a few dollars playing the game, Pop would always ask them…"What's-a-matter with you?" Whether they won or lost, he'd always end the day with, "…and don't tell your mother."

Pop's Driving Now

On another one of those fun trips, Pop and my husband—still a very young boy at the time—were driving along down the road when someone suddenly drove in front of them, completely cutting them off.

Pop's response to this was flipping the guy off and swearing at him. After that ride was over, he ended the trip with his usual, "…and don't tell your mother" speech.

The following week, while riding along in the car with his parents and seeing someone pull in front of them, my husband's innocent child-like response was the same reaction and the very same words that his grandfather had used only a few days prior. This was not received well by his parents, to say the very least. His response to their reaction was, "But Pop did it!"

Later that afternoon, when his grandfather came to visit, his Pop got an earful. Of course, he took it like he always did, with a simple wave of the hand and saying, "Ahhh," like it was no big deal.

Then he ever-so-casually walked over and asked in a semi-quiet voice, "Didn't I tell you not to tell your mother?"

DRIVING LESSONS

Pop would also let my husband practice driving his car when he was young by letting him sit on his lap while driving around in the city. This, of course, wasn't something my mother-in-law approved of. It would never be done today at such a young age, but those were different times.

As they were driving along one day, my husband, who was around twelve years old at the time, somehow ended up driving the car off the road and onto the edge of a cornfield—not too far into it, but just enough.

Pop then started swearing and looked around to see if anyone had seen them. When they didn't see anyone looking, he then told him, "Let's get out of here. If nobody saw it, it didn't happen!"

And that, of course, was also followed by, "...and don't tell your mother."

Another Driving Lesson

This particular driving lesson ended with the car backing into another parked car. This was when my husband was a lot older, and actually had his driving permit.

Pop got out of the car to do a quick inspection. Thankfully, no damage was done. He then looked around to see if anyone had seen what had happened, and once again told him, "If nobody saw you, it didn't happen. Now drive away, and don't tell your mother."

Restaurant Butter is Free?

Living through the Great Depression took its toll on a lot of people. They had to learn how to save money in ways that we just don't do today. Our Pop was no different; he made sure he got his money's worth out of everything. Hmmm...that sounds like someone else I know very well.

One night, our children went out to a local restaurant for dinner with their grandparents and Poppy. As they finished their dinner, they noticed him taking handfuls of the packaged butters that were on the table and stuffing them into his pockets.

Also noticing this was their grandmother, who immediately protested what he was doing. His response was, "Hey, you paid for it—take it!" Their grandmother wasn't too happy about this, but our kids thought it was hysterical.

The only thing their Poppy forgot to add to that little incident was his ever-classic line of, "…and don't tell your mother," because we heard about that story as soon as our kids arrived home.

Chapter Eight

It's All About the Food

Italian Cooking

I didn't grow up with an Italian family or an Italian cooking style at all. We were simply not, in any way, Italian. By the time I reached adult age, I only knew how to make a few, small meals and desserts. The rest, I figured, I'd learn through cookbooks, practice, and experience over the years.

My husband's family and cooking background, however, were very much Italian, and dinners in their home were quite the opposite of ours. After we were married, I was introduced to flavors I never knew existed before. Italian cooking had so much flavor to it—it was wonderful!

Of course, being the novice Italian chef that I was at the time, I decided to try out a new jar of spaghetti sauce while out grocery shopping one day. It was on sale, and with the coupon I had for it, it was almost free, so naturally, I purchased it. How could I pass up such a good deal?

I went home and started to prepare dinner for my family. My husband came home later that evening, smelled dinner cooking, saw the empty jar of sauce, and was *not* happy. He refused to eat the meal I'd prepared, and vowed to have me learn how to make my own sauce from scratch.

Of course, that didn't happen until years later, when I made the mistake of purchasing yet another jar of sauce. It was on sale, and I had a coupon again, so I couldn't resist.

Dinner was prepared again that night, and once more he was not happy. By this time we had children, who were now also confused and appalled by the sauce. That pasta didn't taste like the pasta their Italian grandmother had always made for them.

Our oldest child then called his grandmother and complained.

Soon after that little incident, my husband arranged a day for his grandfather to teach me how to make sauce from scratch. How dare I do it any other way?

After that day, sauce was made from scratch almost every Sunday. It's wonderful; Pop was a wonderful teacher!

I do, however, still occasionally purchase a certain kind of canned pasta in sauce, which one of our children still loves to eat to this day. Unfortunately, this child happened to mention how much they loved that particular pasta while sitting too close to their grandmother one day. The result was a smack upside the head. Canned pasta? Are you kidding? Grandma's homemade sauce is best!

THE ART OF PERSUASION

One year, while we were out and about, enjoying a summer vacation, our family happened to pass a restaurant that is well-known for their ice cream. Although it was local to many areas, it wasn't local to where we lived. Our child, a very young adult at the time, decided it would be fun to stop and try an ice cream, since none of us had ever been there before, and started poking me in the arm while saying the name of the restaurant over and over again, hoping it would convince us to stop.

All three kids thought this was funny, so they all chimed in, chanting the name of the restaurant over and over while continuing to poke me in the arm. By this time, my husband and I were already exhausted from the long day and the lengthy drive. We decided not to stop at that moment, but promised the kids we'd go the following day.

The next day, the very first car ride started out the same way—with all three kids laughing and poking me in the arm, continuously repeating the name of the restaurant over and over. They did this throughout the day, every time we were in the car, until we arrived at that restaurant later that afternoon. Thank God! My arm was killing me.

We got our ice cream to go and started eating it in the car as we drove to our next destination. While we sat there eating, I noticed the children were unusually quiet. Now as a veteran parent, I know that when kids are quiet, it's usually a sign of trouble—unless they're sleeping, of course.

I placed my ice cream down after only having a few bites—it wasn't very good anyway—and I turned around to check on the kids. As I looked back in their direction, I noticed they weren't eating their ice cream as fast as they normally did. One had almost finished his, but the other two were still struggling with theirs.

Oh no! Everyone was getting sick from the ice cream! I could see it on their faces. So I dug out some medication to help ease their stomachs and started handing it out to those who needed it. We then rushed through our last activity for the day and went back to the hotel to rest.

After that day, our kids never did ask to stop at that particular restaurant again. They do, however, still find it funny to poke me in the arm over and over again while repeating the name of other new restaurants they want to try.

Ah, the art of persuasion, and oh, the joys of having three stubborn children who still have yet to understand the concept of karma.

APPLE

For a while, Sunday dinners in our home were always followed with a nice, homemade dessert. This was something our family often looked forward to. Making the decision on what dessert we were going to have was always something we tried to do together.

Trying to get a word in during that conversation, however, could be quite challenging when the kids started spitting out their requests for dessert. They'd all get louder and louder, hoping to be heard and have their selection for dessert chosen for that night.

To avoid what would sometimes end up in a very loud discussion, we'd have a family vote to help make the final decision.

One afternoon, we were all standing around discussing which kind of pie we should make for dessert that night. I was trying to get my point across about an apple pie, but wasn't being heard by anyone. As the conversation continued and the kids got louder and louder, I started repeating myself, hoping to be noticed. I didn't want to yell and bring up the volume of the conversation any further, so I simply repeated the word *apple* over and over again.

It wasn't working.

So I tried a new approach. I continued to repeat myself over and over again; and while doing so, I started to smack my hand against the counter top. I wanted apple pie, damn it, and I wasn't about to yell for it, but I was definitely going to be heard.

This finally got everyone's attention. The kids stopped arguing and then stared at me with looks of total confusion. *Has Mom completely lost her mind?* they wondered. *Oh, I get it now. She wants apple pie! Yup, that's it. What a weird way to ask for apple pie!*

67

Everyone started to laugh at the absurdity of the situation, but my point was made, and I'd finally been heard. Unfortunately, now every time a conversation starts to get loud and someone wants to be heard, they'll all now look at me and start repeating the word *apple* while hitting the countertop. They all think they're so funny!

I also received a fake apple as a Christmas gift last year. Funny little smart asses. I don't know where they get it from.

BABY LETTUCE

It can be difficult to convince a child to try a new vegetable.

We've always made an effort to have our children try at least one bite of anything new. And on some nights, they weren't allowed to have their dessert until they'd tried at least one bite of the new food that was on their plate in front of them.

That worked most of the time, unless it was something that was extremely unappealing to them. In cases like that, my children would actually pass up their dessert to avoid eating it.

One night, we had brussel sprouts with our dinner. The kids all looked at them in confusion, wondering what those horrible-looking balls of green matter were on their plates. I could see it on their faces—they weren't going to try it, no matter what dessert we had planned for the night.

I had to think fast: *What could I do to get them to try brussel sprouts? I got it!*

I told them they were just baby-sized heads of lettuce, and to go ahead and eat them. They all loved the regular-sized ones, so they should like the little ones, as well.

They didn't look too sure about my explanation, because those little things didn't smell like lettuce to them, but they figured Mom wouldn't lie...or would she?

Since they all loved lettuce, it worked great. They still looked confused and unconvinced, but at least they were ready to try them to earn their desserts.

Now, I knew if one of the kids had tried and didn't like their brussel sprouts, the other kids would probably refuse to try theirs. So I told them I'd count to three, and they all had to try them at the same time—together. Consequently, they all popped them into their mouths at the same time.

As fast as the food went in, it all came back out. Children were running for the sink, spitting into their napkins and screaming "Ick!" and "Ewww!" as they ran past me toward the kitchen.

If they'd been allowed to curse at that age, I'm sure I would have heard some of those words, as well.

For some silly reason, they just don't trust me anymore when I try to get them to taste the new foods on their plates.

IT'S A LEMON

Okay, so my children didn't trust me anymore when it came to trying new foods. But they did still trust me with other things, so when I started to cut up a piece of lemon one day, I tried to find a new way to get them to try some.

I absolutely love lemons! I not only enjoy them with my food and in my lemonade and iced tea, I can also sit and eat a piece of one, all by itself, when it's served with just the right entrée.

My kids, however, would never try one on their own. They knew how sour they are, and absolutely refused to try them.

As I cut up a lemon to use with my drink that day, I looked over at my six-year-old and asked her to close her eyes, tip back her head, and open her mouth for a fun surprise.

No problem, she thought—*Mom usually gives us cookie batter to lick off the spatula, popping candy that makes noise when it hits your tongue, or some other sort of fun goodie—so what could go wrong?*

Her head went back and her mouth popped open. *Oh, this is just way too easy,* I thought. *Should I or shouldn't I?*

I couldn't resist. I took half a lemon and squeezed the juice in.

"Acckkk!" She wasn't happy! That wasn't a fun surprise at all.

I started to laugh as she ran past me toward the sink to spit it out.

Oh, the dirty looks I got that day were incredible. I'd finally gotten her to try a lemon, but that was the very last time she ever closed her eyes for a fun surprise. And for some crazy reason, she still doesn't like lemons, to this day…hmm, I wonder why?

YOU STILL HAVE ROOM FOR ONE MORE BITE

Oh, the wonderful challenges of trying to get young children to finish one, small plate of food at dinnertime. Our children, when they were young, would always claim they were way too full to finish their dinner, and couldn't possibly eat one more bite.

Our standing rule in our home was: anyone who didn't finish their dinner, didn't get dessert.

That rule worked quite well, for the most part, but when it didn't, and they still claimed they were way too full to finish their dinners, I'd ask them to lean their heads back and open their mouths wide so I could see if they had any room left.

If I thought they were truly full, I'd tell them they looked full enough, and could go play. If I thought they were just trying to get out of finishing their dinner, I'd tell them they had plenty of room left for a few more bites.

This worked great while they were little. Unfortunately, now that they're older, they don't believe me anymore when I tell them I can see all the way down to their stomachs. I miss that age.

CHAPTER NINE

HOLIDAYS

WHAT KIND OF EGGS DO YOU USE?

We've learned over the years that, when hiding Easter eggs overnight, it's always best to use plastic ones, because there's always that one, last egg that is never found until months later. If we used real eggs, we weren't going to like what we found.

Oh, the horrible stench that comes with finding a two-month-old, hard-boiled egg that has cracked wide open! Eeewww!

Of course, our kids also now prefer plastic eggs—ever since we started filling them with candy and cash, that is. Now, that very last egg that used to take months to discover is most often found within a couple of hours.

The one downside we've found so far to using plastic ones is, if you have a cat that likes to play with noisy things that roll, you'll undoubtedly hear those plastic eggs rolling down the stairs and shattering at the bottom of the staircase. This will usually happen at around 3:00 in the morning. Lesson learned—hide all Easter eggs where the cat can't reach them, or wedge them into a place where he can't pull them out. Otherwise, the children will be awakened by either the eggs crashing at the bottom of the stairs, or Mom and Dad cursing while they run around after the cat.

And no, there's no way to blame the cursing on the bad-tempered Easter bunny. The kids won't buy that story—trust me.

THE BLOODY EASTER EGG HUNT

Easter egg hunts around our house have always been fun. Easter mornings would start out with the kids waking up and checking out their baskets. Then they'd start peeking around, searching for eggs, even though they knew it wasn't time to start looking just yet.

Once this started, we'd give them the go-ahead to start their search. Over the years, as our kids have grown and the cash inside the eggs has increased, it has literally become a blood sport. Now they run, push, and shove one another to get to the eggs, laughing the entire time.

One Easter, not too long ago, there was a little bit of blood involved, as our newest family member—our German shepherd—decided to get in on the action. Amidst the running, yelling, shoving, and laughter, she decided that she needed to get involved and help out. At one point, she jumped on top of one child who'd pushed and shoved another child. In doing so, she inadvertently scratched the one she was trying to protect.

As the kids continued their wild behavior, running, pushing, and shoving each other, she continued to try to protect those that she thought needed it. She jumped over the couch several times, going after our oldest son and trying to protect our daughter. She even tore his shirt wide open in the process.

By the end of the egg hunt, the kids all sat around the kitchen table, bloody, bruised, scratched, and out of breath, laughing like crazy as they counted their eggs, goodies, and cash to see who'd found the most.

The funniest part was that the most aggressive child ended up with the most scratches, a shirt that was half torn off, and the least amount of cash.

I can't believe how dangerous our simple, little Easter egg hunts have become over the years. It truly has become an actual blood sport.

THE NIGHT BEFORE CHRISTMAS

This was a wonderful time for our kids, as the excitement always grew with the anticipation of Christmas Day. In our home on Christmas Eve, each person in our family was allowed to open one present.

This was a lot of fun, and something our kids always looked forward to. They couldn't wait to start opening their gifts, and would set aside each of their presents a few days ahead of time so they knew right where they were. Then they'd shake each one, trying to guess what was inside.

Since we knew they'd be thoroughly inspecting each and every present, we came up with a few ways to disguise what was inside. We'd add rocks to disguise the actual weight, fill one box after another to make a small present seem large, and even stuff the side of the box with odd-shaped pieces of cardboard to make the shape of it more difficult to decipher. As the children have learned over the years, looks, sounds, and weights can be quite deceiving.

One child discovered this when they chose to open an extra-large present, thinking it was going to be the one they'd been hoping for. Instead they discovered a box filled to the brim with their not-so-favorite item…clothes. We'd wrapped them in an extra-large carton, almost the size of the child we were giving it to, and then placed a few heavy rocks at the bottom to add to the weight, so they wouldn't be able to tell it was only clothing.

Of course, we had the actual present they were looking for hidden away in another room, but we didn't mention that. We brought that one out Christmas morning.

There's nothing more entertaining than seeing a child's face Christmas morning when they realize they did indeed receive what they'd asked for. Ah, it's so much fun to mess with kids during the holidays.

Toilet Paper?

Christmas in our home has always been a lot of fun. When it came time to give gifts, we always tried to make unwrapping our presents as entertaining as possible. If we could think of a way to mess with each other, we did. As a result of that, gift-giving on Christmas has always been entertaining, to say the least.

Adding rocks to the bottom of our gifts to disguise the actual weight of the present wasn't the only thing we'd do. Our kids would open presents and find one, small piece of paper inside with a clue written on it, that led to another piece of paper with a clue on it, that led to another piece of paper, and so on, until the present was finally found.

They loved these little treasure hunts when they were young, but not so much anymore. We've also wrapped presents in box after box after box, until they'd unwrapped up to ten different boxes before reaching the actual gift itself. We've sealed presents shut with thick amounts of shipping tape that could never be undone. Those had to be cut open. And we've wrapped an extra-large box that had only one, very small box inside.

The best gift of all was given to one lucky child, who unwrapped his gift and looked utterly confused as he pulled it out of the box—a roll of toilet paper. On this roll of toilet paper, I'd written an extremely long letter that was the entire length of the toilet paper roll.

To give a brief description of what was said, it basically just kept asking him over and over again if he was ready to receive his real gift, and went on to say just how exciting it was, and how special it was, and "here it is," and "oh, wait a minute, not yet," and so on. At the end of the roll was the actual present—cash for a new laptop for college, tucked deep inside the roll. It took a long time for him to get to the actual present, but he thought it was worth it in the end.

THE GIFT OF LOVE

On one particular Christmas, my husband and I agreed to limit the amount we were going to spend on one another. It was something we'd done in the past, and it had worked out very well, so we decided to try it again that year.

We also tried to keep things fair by giving each other the same number of gifts. This was always his favorite part of the agreement, as he'd always one-up me with that one, extra, last-minute gift.

As usual, he tried to pull that little trick again that year. He was smiling, thinking he'd won again, as he placed that one, last gift under the tree on Christmas Eve. As I saw him doing this, I decided it was finally time to get even.

On Christmas morning, just as the last present was being unwrapped, I pulled out one last gift I'd hidden for him inside the branches of our Christmas tree. It was a small gift, but it was just enough to keep us even.

He wasn't happy, because he thought I'd broken our agreement and spent more money trying to even things up, but I promised him that I didn't go over the spending limit. I told him to go ahead and open it.

He didn't look too convinced, but decided to open it anyway.

As he opened his present and looked inside, he started to look a bit confused. At the bottom, lying inside the box, was a tiny piece of paper cut into the shape of a heart. As he lifted the paper heart out of the box, he asked me what it was supposed to be.

I told him it was a box full of love, just for him.

That'll teach him. I kept within the rules of our agreement and didn't spend any more money than I'd promised. The kids thought it was hysterical, but he just wasn't feeling the love.

SATAN FOR CHRISTMAS?

Okay, so I've already said my children think it's weird that their mother likes to listen to hard rock and heavy metal music, and because of that, they like to tease me by telling people that I'm the devil in disguise. Well, this teasing happens all year long, and believe me, our family continues to torture each other right through the holidays. Sometimes, that's when we get the most creative and start to put some real thought and effort into it.

One Christmas morning, as we were all sitting around opening our gifts, I noticed a strange-looking present tucked way under the tree. It had my name on it, and was from one of the kids. This particular child had obviously done some extra work to mess with me that year. They'd chosen a bright-red gift bag and drawn a satanic symbol with a black marker on the side. I picked it up and started to look over the bag carefully. *This is going to be interesting, to say the least,* I mused. *What did this child do?*

As I started to open the gift, everyone else stopped unwrapping their presents to watch me open mine. This child was now grinning from ear-to-ear.

Oh no, I thought. *Should I even open it? What did he do? Is something going to jump out at me?*

I worked slowly and carefully as I peeled back the massive amounts of tape used to hold it closed. I then opened the bag and ever-so-gently pushed back the tissue paper to look inside. Inside was a satanic bible and a homemade wooden cross that had been spray-painted black with red satanic symbols drawn all over it.

Wow. He'd put a lot of time and effort into this little prank! I was impressed. A little concerned, receiving such a satanic gift on such a holy day, but still quite impressed with the effort.

I looked up in amazement at my son's face, which was now beaming with pride at the wonderful joke he'd just played on his mother. I asked what I was supposed to do with the wonderful gift he'd just given me.

As an even bigger smile washed over his face, he then responded, "You can use them to chase off the Jehovah's Witness people that keep stopping by, trying to convert you."

Okay, he got an A+ for that one.

IT'S TRADITION

Is it really necessary to get a real, live tree every year for Christmas? My children and I think so. They all look forward to throwing snowballs at one another and making snow angels as we hike around in the woods looking for the perfect one each year. We also enjoy the smell of these trees during the holidays. Although my husband also appreciates this smell, he doesn't appreciate the process we go through every year to get one. He always protests and asks why we can't use a fake one instead. Then the kids and I will argue, "Because, it's tradition!"

One year we gathered the family, jumped into the car, and drove to a local tree farm to find the perfect Christmas tree. What an event it was that year.

We hiked all over for about an hour or more, so the kids could find the largest, most perfect-looking tree they could agree on. Once they found what they thought was the perfect one, their father—as he does every year—started to sigh and shake his head as he tried to convince them to find something smaller.

They protested as usual saying, "But it's tradition; we have to get a big one!"

At that point, I could no longer feel my toes. I told my husband I was now officially frozen and asked him if we could please just get the tree they'd chosen.

Seeing he was outnumbered yet again, he gave up and helped us decide whose turn it was to help him cut down the tree. After the tree was cut down, he and our oldest son started dragging it up the hill toward our vehicle. Yes, this extra-large, heavy tree was found at the bottom of a very large hill once again that year.

They stopped to take breaks, because dragging that heavy tree up the steep hill was no easy task. Each time they stopped, they'd glare at the rest of us following behind them and we would all start to snicker.

As they pulled the tree along, their father was now starting to mumble, asking why we'd chosen yet another large, heavy tree at the bottom of the hill once again. No one had an answer for him, other than to say, "Because, that's where all the good ones always are."

And why was that the area where all the good ones were always found? Well, according to my husband, it was, "Because no one else wanted to haul those big a**, heavy trees up that blankety-blank hill—that's why!"

It's usually at this point when my husband starts to swear, and we all have trouble holding back our laughter. We then try to help out a bit by attempting to carry the other end of the tree but that usually just agitates him even more, which is quite frankly…even funnier.

Once we reached the top of the hill, we now had to try to figure out how to place our extra-large tree on top of our vehicle without doing any damage to any family members, the tree, or the vehicle itself. As my husband sized up the tree and then looked at our vehicle, he started to curse all over again. How were we going to get something that big up over our heads and onto the roof of our SUV?

After a few more choice words, he started cutting a little more off the bottom of the tree, hoping it would help. As he was doing this, other people were now walking by with their much-smaller trees, making comments about how large ours was. That wasn't helping at all.

This happened almost every year, and almost every time, he'd glare at me and the kids and make some sort of comment about how nice the other people's tree had looked and how ridiculous and unnecessary it was to get a tree as big as the one we'd chosen.

Of course, by this time, the kids and I were already starting to giggle a bit at his obvious show of frustration.

A few minutes later, we had somehow managed to get the tree on top of our vehicle, but it still needed to be tied down. My husband started cursing once again as he tried to throw ropes over and around the tree. It was not working very well, and he was getting stabbed with needles as he tried to do it.

The rest of us were now laughing out loud while exchanging looks of fear as we tried desperately to help, while still staying out of the way of this cursing man and the ropes that were being tossed into the air.

This was the most entertaining part of getting a Christmas tree every year—watching Dad flip out while trying to get an oversized Christmas tree attached to our vehicle.

After about twenty minutes or so of laughing, cursing, tugging, and tying ropes together, we were finally ready for the drive home. On the way, chocolate goodies and candy canes were tossed around to each child. We all took turns peeking out the windows to check on the tree.

Everyone was happy, until they started to thaw out. Oh, the pain that comes with thawing feet and hands. There were a few minor complaints and laughing as the thawing continued, and then several requests for more goodies by the time we arrived home.

We got out and immediately checked on the tree. Wow. We'd made it home, and the tree was still in place. Well, maybe a few inches farther back from where we'd originally placed it, but it was still there and hanging on.

The kids were getting more excited now. Yay! We were finally home. Time to eat dinner and decorate the tree.

As my husband and our oldest untied the tree and dragged it over to our back door, the rest of us started moving furniture around to make room. Once they reached the back door, I heard the mumbling of curse words yet again. Obviously, the tree was still a little too big to fit through our double doors. So he cut a little more off the bottom once more, and then somehow managed to squeeze it through the door.

I walked behind them, cleaning up the trail of needles and melting snow as they dragged the tree through our living room, placed the stand on the bottom, and tried to stand it up.

My husband was getting stabbed with needles while trying to steady the tree. As he was doing this, he looked up and noticed the mark on the ceiling that the tree had just made when he'd tried to stand it up.

The top of the tree was now bending over as it pressed against the ceiling. He knew he'd have to trim it once more.

He made a quick comment about the mark that had been made, and how ridiculous it was to get a tree that big. Then, he held the tree in place while I crawled underneath to screw in the stand.

Okay, time to see if it worked. He let go of the tree. I stayed on the floor, waiting for more instructions. As soon as he released it, it immediately started to tip forward. He quickly grabbed it and asked me to make another adjustment to the tree stand.

I made the adjustment and we tried it once again. The tree was still crooked. So I made another adjustment and the tree was still crooked. One more adjustment, and the tree finally stood on its own.

The top of the tree was then trimmed, so it was no longer touching the ceiling. Then we started to gather the lights and ornaments needed to decorate it.

The kids were excited now, and had already started looking for their favorite ornaments. As they were doing this, the tree started to lean once more. My husband ran over and grabbed the tree to keep it from falling.

Now covered in sap while being stabbed by needles, he started cursing all over again. He then gave me a nasty look and told me he was now going to screw in the tree stand himself—the right way.

Being covered with sap and needles myself from being underneath the tree earlier, I had no problem telling him to go ahead and try, as I took a turn holding the tree in place.

After another adjustment, the tree was still crooked. We made another one, and the tree was once again standing on its own. *Good enough*, we thought.

I then retrieved some water from the kitchen and crawled back under the tree to fill the stand. I couldn't believe it—the water was going down a bit faster than usual.

Just as I announced to my family that this particular tree was really thirsty this year, water started to leak out from under the tree stand.

The kids started to laugh as they realized their mother had just had a very blonde moment. The tree stand evidently had a small crack in the bottom, and was now slowly and steadily leaking water all over the floor.

We mopped up the water and took down the tree. We put it in a new tree stand and screwed it in. Then, after a few more adjustments and a bit more cursing out of my husband, the tree was finally standing on its own once again.

The tree was up; now it was time to relax a bit and enjoy our evening.

Our children found the movie that our family has watched every year since they were little, and started to play it as we began to decorate the tree.

As the movie continued to play, I started setting out a few appetizers and finished preparing dinner, while everyone else finished decorating the tree. A ham had been cooking throughout the day while we were gone, and it was just about done. Oh, the delightful aromas that come from a ham dinner and a freshly cut pine tree—it was wonderful.

After an hour or so, the tree was fully decorated and dinner was finally done. How beautiful the tree looked, and what a nice meal we all had in front of us.

At last, we were able to sit down to relax and enjoy our wonderful meal and the movie that was still playing. There were a few comments on how beautiful the new Christmas tree was, and how much fun we'd all had getting yet another oversized Christmas tree that day. Even my husband, at that point, was starting to laugh about the oversized tree we'd chosen.

As we sat around enjoying the wonderful, relaxing evening we were finally having, I couldn't help but think about how blessed we all were, and what a wonderful day it had been, spending quality time together.

At that very moment, the tree fell over yet again, spilling water everywhere, smashing countless decorations, and scaring the hell out of the cat, who had apparently been behind the tree checking it out.

The cat took off running, my husband started to curse once again, and the kids and I all burst into laughter. Silly me—I'd thought we were going to have a nice, quiet, uneventful evening for once.

We picked up the tree, tied it to the wall, cleaned up the mess, banished the cat, and then sat back down to finish our dinner.

We now tie our Christmas trees to the wall every year; it's just a part of our wonderful Christmas tree tradition. Ah, the joys of Christmas.

CHAPTER TEN

OUCH!

INSTALLING NEW CARPET

O ne summer day years ago, we were in our child's bedroom looking at the carpet. After giving it a thorough inspection, we came to the conclusion that it needed to be replaced.

The next day, we drove to a local flooring company to find a suitable replacement for it. After looking at several pieces, we finally chose one and made our purchase.

As we finished paying for our new carpet, we were asked whether we wanted the company to install it for us. My husband decided he didn't want to spend any extra money on installation costs. He'd install it himself, with the help of his father. So we brought the carpet home and made a call to my father-in-law for help.

As they worked together, my husband knelt down to start cutting off a piece of carpet using a box-cutting blade.

My father-in-law walked behind him and tripped over his ankles. That caused my husband's hand—the one with the blade still in it—to jolt forward, slicing his adjacent wrist.

The cut was fairly deep and was bleeding quite extensively, so he asked me to help bandage the wound. Then he went back to work on the carpet installation.

Later that night, he asked me to change the bandage and check on his wound. As I carefully tried to pull off the bandage, something kept holding it in place—it just wouldn't come off. At this point, he wasn't enjoying what I was doing at all, and asked me to please hurry and just quickly pull it off.

I gave it a quick yank, and he let out a scream. Apparently, the bandage was still attached to the wound itself, and I'd just torn open his wrist even more when I pulled it off.

As a result of this little incident, I had to drive my husband to the emergency room for stitches and stand there while he described to the doctor, in full detail, how I'd ripped open his wrist.

Oops.

A New Basketball Hoop

When our son was nine years old, he decided he wanted a basketball hoop to play with outside. Thinking that would be a great thing for him to have, we all decided to go shopping together to pick one out.

After a few minutes of searching, we found one we thought was perfect. It was mounted on its own stand and was portable, so we wouldn't have to place it anywhere permanently.

We purchased it right away and then headed for home. Once we were home, we opened the box and discovered a very lengthy set of instructions. After reviewing the instructions, we decided the best place for assembly was on a concrete pad in the back yard, where the surface would be easiest to work on.

As we worked on putting our new purchase together, our son was bouncing around the base of it, getting more and more excited. He just couldn't wait—it was almost done.

At the very end of the instructions, we learned that we were supposed to place sand in the base of it. As we were reviewing the instructions, the basketball hoop started to fall over from the lack of weight in the base.

We saw this starting to happen, in what seemed like a horrible, slow-motion kind of movement. We both yelled for our son to get out of the way.

Unfortunately, both of us were just out of reach and couldn't make it in time to catch it. The hoop landed directly on top of him, knocking him face-first into the concrete surface.

He was a bit stunned by the blow. We brought him into the house to check for injuries.

After a few minutes, he started to realize what had happened, and then couldn't understand why we were trying to get him to sit still for a few minutes when there was a brand-new basketball hoop outside to play with.

The injuries for that day included one severely scraped, bloody, and bruised nose on the face of a child who *still* wanted to play basketball.

Sunburn and a Swollen Eye

One morning, my husband took our son to visit some friends at a nearby lake to fish, swim, and do lots of other fun outdoor activities. For once, he actually remembered to tell him to put on sunblock before the day even started. He smeared it on, and my husband even helped place some of it on his back to get full coverage.

Once the sunblock was applied, they set out for the day. They fished, swam, and played all morning long in the sun. What a beautiful day it was.

When they arrived back home, I took one look at our son and asked my husband, "What in the hell happened to him?"

"Why—what's wrong?" he responded. Then he took one look and instantly noticed the problem. Our son's right eye was severely swollen, and massive sunburn was starting to form all over his body.

Evidently, the sunblock was not waterproof, and was never reapplied after they'd gone swimming. Then, while driving home with the window wide open, our son had enjoyed the nice breeze in his face, resulting in pollen accumulation in his right eye. That left it extremely swollen from a response to allergies.

The poor kid looked like a lobster that had been punched in the eye. He had second-degree sunburn and a bad allergic reaction, all at the same time.

I gave him a dose of aspirin right away and told him to go take a cold shower to help ease what was obviously not going to be a comfortable night for him.

The swollen eye went down later that night, but the sunburn turned more and more red as it settled into his skin. Over the next week or so, blisters started to form and his skin started to peel. He had to rest and avoid being outside.

Needless to say, our son now uses sunblock on a somewhat regular basis, and my husband now checks to make sure he's reapplied it, both before and after swimming. On the days when he doesn't want to bother with it, all I have to do is show him the picture I took of him looking like the one-eyed lobster boy. It works every time. I knew that picture would come in handy.

HOW DOES THAT WORK?

When our son was around four years old, he had a fascination with learning how to fix things. We'd often find him taking toys apart as he'd try to figure out how each one worked.

To encourage his curiosity and help him continue learning how to fix things, we purchased a toy workbench and tool set for him to play with. He was so cute with it; he'd help me and his dad fix things around the house all the time.

As he was quietly playing in his bedroom one morning, for some reason or another, the heat register dial caught his attention. Apparently, it looked like it needed to be taken apart and fixed, but the tools we'd given him to play with just weren't going to do the job.

As soon as I wasn't paying attention, he retrieved a screwdriver from the adult set of tools and started to pry it open.

As he was doing this, I was running around the house, cleaning and picking up, thinking he was still playing with the toys in his room. I didn't have a clue what he was up to until I suddenly noticed the lights go out and then flicker back on again.

As this happened, I also heard a loud thump in my son's bedroom.

I quickly ran upstairs to see what the noise was. The first thing I saw was him sitting on the floor with a screwdriver in his hand, looking a bit dazed and confused.

"What happened?" I asked. "What are you doing with the screwdriver?"

He never did get a chance to answer me before I noticed the large, black mark on the wall. That black mark spoke volumes as to what had happened.

Unfortunately for him, upon sticking the screwdriver into the heat register casing, he'd touched some wiring and received a very strong electrical shock that sent him flying across the room. Thank God for auto shut-off and surge protection. It could have been a lot worse.

Needless to say, we now keep all tools away from this child who, quite frankly, is no longer interested in how electrical things work anyway.

YOU SHOULD HAVE CHANGED THE TOILET PAPER ROLL!

One day our son went to use the bathroom, only to discover a little too late that, yet again, someone had used up all the toilet paper and hadn't bothered to change the roll. He wasn't too happy, and started yelling for his sister who, he assumed, had left it that way. He told her to change the roll immediately.

Our daughter, while laughing hysterically, ran to retrieve a new roll, but as she ran past the stairway, he assumed she was running away from the situation. So he ran up the stairs, grabbed her by the ankles, and then proceeded to drag her down the stairs on her rear end.

As she bounced off each and every step along the way, she was no longer laughing. Her butt was now very bruised and sore.

After a few choice words between the two of them, our son simply stated to her, as he casually walked away, "Well, you should've changed the toilet paper roll!"

The toilet paper rolls in our home are now changed a lot more often. Now if I could only keep the empty rolls off the floor, and the toilet paper dispensing in the right direction.

LIGHTING THE SMOKER

Time to light the smoker for another wonderful summertime barbecue. My husband got out the usual supplies, set everything in place, and started to light the fire inside the smoker.

I cautioned him, as I do every year, to be careful and keep the fire from getting too big. He told me not to worry about it, and then proceeded to build what he thought was a very nice fire.

A little while later, as the fire started to permeate the air with that wonderful backyard-barbecue smell; he decided it was time to check on the smoker to see if it was ready for the food to be placed inside. As he opened the side door of the smoker to check on the coals, he was greeted with a large wall of flames, which instantly scorched the hair on the sides of his legs.

He jumped back and closed the door as fast as he could, then started to inspect his legs. He was okay, but his legs were a bit red from the heat and the hair on his legs was entirely burned off.

"Are you okay?" I asked, trying unsuccessfully to hold back my laughter. He shot me a dirty look. Saying, "I told you so" is so hard to do when you can't stop laughing.

It took weeks before the hair grew back on his legs.

WAXING THE STAIRS

Ah, cleaning day…it was one of those days when I looked around at the mess in my home and the kids who were sitting around complaining about how bored they were, and I decided it was time for them to help clean up the mess they'd helped create.

Even though our children didn't always do the best job when they cleaned, we always thought it was very important to have them learn how to be responsible for cleaning up around the house they lived in. In doing so, they'd also learn how to do the job correctly.

I'd learned over the years that if I have kids redo a task they hadn't done very well in the first place, they quickly learn how to do it right the first time. So on that day, I gave each child a list of things to do and told them to take their time and do a nice job on each one, or they'd be doing it a second time.

All three children agreed to work real hard. They were soon off and running with their lists of things to do.

I was very impressed; they were actually taking the time to do each job well. I was so proud!

I noticed one particular child working extra hard on our oak staircase. I'd told them to simply wipe it down with a wet rag; they'd taken the extra step of getting out the wood polish to help make it shine. Our stairs looked beautiful.

Ah, the wonderful feeling of children helping to clean the house the right way, and oh, the beauty of a nicely waxed oak staircase. The child who cleaned it was so proud of the job that was done.

Then, along came another one to see what all the fuss was about. Wasn't it beautiful?

Oh, and there they go, bouncing down the stairs. I guess it's better not to wax the stairs. Guess we won't do that again.

ICE-HILL SLEDDING

Time for some wintertime fun outside. The kids were so excited—they finally had a day off from school because of all the nasty weather we'd had overnight. Now they were looking forward to playing outside in the snow, and we had plenty of it.

But along with all that snow came a lot of freezing rain as well. That freezing rain had also left behind a thick layer of ice that had blanketed the snow and the entire hill behind our home.

The sunlight shining off of the ice that day was absolutely beautiful. The children noticed it instantly and decided it would be perfect for sliding. After breakfast, they got dressed and hurried out the door to play.

They ran around for a while, having fun slipping and sliding, trying to maneuver themselves up and down the hill. They'd slide quickly down and then spend a long time punching through the ice with their hands and feet as they tried to crawl their way back up the hill.

At one point, our son was punching through the snow and ice as hard as he could, trying desperately to make his way back up the hill. As he did this, his boot suddenly slipped on the ice and flew backward, hitting his sister, who'd been crawling up the hill directly behind him. She hadn't been paying attention to how close she was, and caught the flying boot directly in the mouth.

As she started screaming, our son turned around to see what happened. In doing so, he slipped and smacked his face on the ice.

Results of the day: One massive, bloody mess on the beautiful ice formation outdoors, a trail of blood leading to our back door from a bleeding nose and two battered and bloody-faced children who decided that sitting inside, drinking hot chocolate through straws—much easier to do with two fat lips—was much better than bloody ice-hill sledding.

Years later, as we recalled that story, my kids said to me, "Yeah, we probably should've gone around the ice to get up the hill instead."

Sure—now they think of that!

HOT PEPPERS ARE SO GOOD!

Why do people insist on eating hot foods that make them turn red and start to sweat? Is it the flavor, or the actual challenge they enjoy most?

I personally don't understand how anyone can enjoy the flavor of any food when they're burning up inside and out.

My husband is one of those people—he just loves to eat hot peppers, and can usually handle them without even breaking a sweat.

While working in the garden one afternoon, we noticed the hot peppers we'd been growing all summer long were finally ready for harvesting. They were beautiful—nice and big and just right for picking. So we gathered them up, finished our chores for the day, and headed inside.

After the peppers had been thoroughly washed, my husband decided to try a few of them before dinner, while they were still fresh. He took out his usual goodies to go with them—crackers, cheese, and olives—sliced the peppers to just the right thickness, and then put them all together to make a cracker sandwich.

It looked delicious, but I knew better than to attempt taking a bite, as I'd had these peppers before. It hadn't been a pleasant experience, to say the least. So I decided to rest in the chair for a minute while I watched him eat them.

Those particular peppers were a little hotter than usual. He took one bite and immediately started to sweat. As he ate, his face turned redder and redder. The beads of sweat started to form on his forehead.

"These peppers are so good!" he proclaimed. I watched in amazement, not understanding how he was able to accomplish swallowing those little balls of fire.

After he finished his snack, he decided it was a good time to get in a quick shower before dinner and after working in the garden under the hot sun for most of the day. I agreed that was a good idea.

A few minutes had passed when I heard the water for the shower running. The next noise I heard was my husband screaming. I ran in to see what the problem was.

"My eyes! My eyes!" he yelled.

Apparently, it's not a good idea to attempt washing your hair with the same hands that recently cut up a batch of newly picked, extra-hot peppers.

WALK THE DOGS

A few days after adopting our new dog from a local animal shelter, my husband and I decided it was time to take her out for a walk to see how she'd do.

She was a sweet, young German shepherd that was beyond skinny when we'd first found her, but was now gaining weight and starting to look a bit stronger and healthier each day. We figured it was a good time to see just how healthy she really was.

Our son, who was around eleven years old at the time, decided he wanted to go with us so he could be the first one to walk our new dog for the very first time. We gathered the dog leashes and both dogs, including our older dog, a black Labrador, and headed out the door.

As we started our walk, we noticed that both dogs were competing with each other to take the lead. We'd pull on their leashes to slow them down a bit, and then they'd run to get in front of each other, over and over again. They continued this awkward walking pattern until it was time to head back home. This was our older dog's favorite part of our walks, as she always enjoyed sprinting that last mile toward home.

As we made our way down the hill, our new dog noticed a deer in the middle of the road a few yards away. She suddenly bolted in its direction. This, in turn, had our older dog thinking it was time to run home, so she started running as well.

Our son, who was still holding on to the leash of our new dog, was entirely caught off guard. He was instantly thrown into the air by the force of this now-very-strong and healthy German shepherd, who'd taken off running. He flew several feet into the air before making a crash landing, scraping his chin and elbow along the dirt road.

We watched in amazement as the dust flew up in the air from the force of our child landing on the road as he tried desperately to hang on.

My husband and I ran after them as quickly as we could, yelling for both dogs to stop. Our son was still hanging on to the leash, and the dog was still trying to run.

It took a minute or so, but once we had both dogs stopped and under control, we checked for injuries. Our son was mad, and a bit scraped up on his elbow and chin, but otherwise okay. Our dogs however, were a bit confused by all the commotion.

Everyone, for the most part, was okay. Now it was time to start laughing. Oh, my word! The sight of a child flying in mid-air like that, above an overly excited dog who was running at absolute full speed, was enough to keep us laughing for the rest of our walk home.

Our son didn't find it very humorous that day, but we found it hysterical.

LET'S BUILD A FORT

One sunny afternoon, our son was playing in the backyard when he somehow came to the conclusion that he needed a fort to play in. We sat and discussed where and how to build it, then drew up a set of plans to work off of.

My husband and I gathered the tools and the supplies we needed and headed outside to get started on it.

We spent several days working on it together. Our son couldn't wait until it was done; he was so excited!

As we were working on it one afternoon, my husband decided that one of the posts hadn't been placed quite deep enough into the ground. Just as I walked over to see what he was doing and ask whether I could help, he lifted up the post, which was attached to a two-by-four board that was now above my head, and proceeded to slam it back into the ground.

Subsequently, that same two-by-four board that was attached to the post slammed down directly onto my head.

105

"Stop!" I yelled. My head was now in terrible pain.

As he turned around, he instantly knew what had happened. He took one look at me and decided we should go to the emergency room right away.

I was already starting to feel nauseated and a little lightheaded, so I reluctantly agreed to go. While we were getting ready to leave, our kids decided they wanted to tag along for the ride. They jumped in the car with us, and off we went.

A few minutes later, we arrived at the emergency room and made our way up to the receptionist's window. I noticed the nurses sitting around in the background, waiting for the next patient to arrive. Thankfully, it was a very slow night for them, so I wouldn't have to wait too long to be seen.

Since my husband was feeling horribly guilty about the accident that had just occurred, and since I was still conscious and breathing, I decided to have a little fun with the situation to help lighten the mood. As I stood there at the receptionist window, I told the lady that my husband had just hit me in the head with a two-by-four board and I needed to be seen by a doctor as soon as possible. I didn't bother to mention that it had been an accident.

The entire staff, completely caught off guard by what I'd said, stopped what they were doing, looked at me and then my husband, then at each other, and then back at me again.

Apparently, telling an emergency room staff that you were hit by your husband with a two-by-four is a huge cause for concern and a whole lot of paperwork.

My kids and I found it funny, as did the emergency room staff, after I explained that it was, indeed, an accident, but my husband didn't find it funny at all. I guess he was remembering the emergency room incident we'd dealt with years before, when we were separated by staff members so they could find out whether I was being abused. I'll tell that little story in a minute, but first let me tell about my second concussion.

THE HAZARDS OF FEEDING CHICKENS

Where we live, lots of people have chickens. I know that's not very normal for most people, but the fresh eggs are something my family truly enjoys.

One winter day I threw on my coat and boots, grabbed the snacks for the chickens, and headed out the door. I walked outside onto the grassy area of the lawn, trying to avoid the ice that had developed in the driveway overnight. As I walked through the thin blanket of snow on the lawn, I failed to see the ice patch that was hidden underneath.

As soon as my feet hit this ice patch, I slipped and fell, landing flat on my back and slamming my head onto the hard, frozen ground.

I was instantly nauseated and dizzy. I was having a little trouble catching my breath, but I still somehow managed to get up and walk back inside the house for a minute.

I was pissed. The snacks for the chickens were all over the ground outside, and I was now going to be late for work because I had to take time to gather myself together, recuperate a bit from the incident, and then try to go back outside to clean up my mess and finish the job I'd started.

Our son saw me come back inside and noticed I wasn't looking very well. I told him I'd fallen and hit my head and was hurt, but I should be fine in a minute or so. However, if I didn't come back inside the house within my usual time, he should come check on me to make sure I wasn't passed out somewhere in the snow.

He laughed and told me maybe that wasn't such a good idea in my condition, but I decided to try it anyway. I did manage to finish feeding the chickens, but they received the express version of care that morning.

By the time I got to work that day, I was still very nauseated, had a horrible headache, and couldn't read the computer screen at all.

I'd only been there for a few minutes when my coworkers convinced me to go to the emergency room.

I wasn't happy about having to go, but was starting to realize it was probably a good idea to get checked out, since I was now having trouble with my vision.

After my doctor reviewed my chart and read about the previous concussion I'd sustained only six months earlier, he ordered a few tests and gave me a speech about how I should really try harder to stop hitting my head.

Gee, I don't remember throwing myself to the ground on purpose, I thought to myself. *Let me see if I can manage that!*

I went home and told my husband what had happened and what the doctor had told me to do. In response, he offered to buy me a pretty blue helmet. Ha, ha, ha. Very funny.

The result of this little incident was my second concussion within a six-month period, a bruise on my rear end from the cell phone that had been in my back pocket at the time, migraines for months, test after test given by doctors for the next two years, and forever being reminded by doctors and family members to stop hitting my head. Damn chickens.

Now for the, story about how my husband and I were separated at an emergency room to make sure I wasn't being abused:

I BROKE MY A-s-s!

A broken tailbone hurts like crazy, and is a horribly embarrassing place to have an injury. I literally broke mine not just once, but twice.

The first incident happened over twenty years ago, back in July of 1991. My husband and I were playing around one night, giving each other little punches and kicks. I'd punch; he'd punch back. He'd kick; I'd kick back. This went on for a few minutes, until he decided to give me one good, swift kick in the ass—literally.

He was barefoot at the time, and we weren't trying to hurt each other—we were just playing around—so I wouldn't have expected it to be that bad, but somehow he managed to catch me just right.

The next thing I knew, I couldn't move. He couldn't believe what he'd just done.

We went to the emergency room and explained what happened, and were immediately separated into two different rooms by the emergency room staff.

If I hadn't been in so much pain that day, I could have had a lot of fun with that one, as the staff had to interrogate him to make sure I wasn't being abused. But we finally convinced them it was, indeed, an accident. Finally they let him come back in the room with me and continued with the exam and X-rays.

The X-ray showed a break in my tailbone, which was now pointing inward instead of downward. They told me there was nothing they could do to reset the bone—I'd have to put up with the pain for a few weeks until it healed.

For the next few weeks, I was walking a little slower, sitting in a somewhat tilted manner, and every time I'd sneeze, I'd make this sound: "Achoo—ow! Achoo—ow! Achoo—ow!" It hurt like hell to sneeze, but it made everyone around me laugh like crazy.

The second time I injured my tailbone was in July of 2012. It had been a long summer, with many wasp and bee problems, and we'd disassembled more nests than we could keep track of.

It had now gotten to the point where we were starting to do daily inspections to try to keep up with the problem. It was unbelievable how many we found.

As I was doing my routine inspection one day, I came across a new nest starting to form underneath the peak of the rooftop on our home. Since we'd had so many bee attacks on us and our pets over the past two years, I decided it was time to get this one down before it was too big to handle.

I told my husband I was going outside to disassemble yet another wasp nest. He decided he'd come out to watch, in case I needed any help.

I retrieved a tall ladder and a long-handled tool from the garage, and we both headed outside toward the nest. I placed the ladder underneath it and started to climb up, determined to get them before they got us once more.

My husband didn't want to get too close to the wasps, in case they got mad and attacked, so he didn't bother holding the ladder for me this time. Instead, he stood back, far out of the way, and laughed, saying, "This ought to be good—let's see what happens."

As I started to poke at the nest with the long-handled tool, I noticed there were only three or four wasps flying around it. I was relieved to see it wasn't that active yet.

I continued to poke at it with the handle until it was totally crushed. Fortunately, it was still fairly small in size, so it didn't take too long to get it down.

Once the nest was destroyed and had fallen to the ground, I started down the ladder. There were only a few wasps left that were still flying around above me, looking for their home, so I wasn't too concerned about being stung.

As I stepped down the ladder, I was still watching the situation above me and wasn't paying attention to where my feet were. As a result, I missed a step, lost my balance, and fell about fifteen feet to the ground. I landed right on my back and tailbone.

My head, although it didn't hit the ground, was also shaken pretty badly, rudely awakening the two concussions I'd received two years prior. I guess I might need that pretty blue helmet after all.

As soon as I hit the ground, I was instantly in pain and a little dizzy, but most of all, not happy about falling off the ladder. At least I'd gotten the wasp nest down, damn it!

As my husband rushed over to see if I was okay, I tried to get up on my own, but was having a bit of trouble, as my body was refusing to move at first.

He helped me up, and as he did, he started laughing as he told me, "You actually bounced off the ground!"

Well...that would explain why he was laughing so hard.

I never did go to the emergency room to get my tailbone checked out again, so I'm not a hundred percent sure it was re-broken, but based on the position it's now in, I'm going to go ahead and guess that it was indeed broken once more.

I know I probably should have gone to get checked out, but I wasn't about to go to the doctor for yet another head and tailbone injury! They'd seen me enough over the past two years for those types of injuries, and I wasn't going to waste any more money on yet another doctor's visit that was only going to lead to more tests and another lecture on how I need to be more careful.

There was nothing they could do for my injuries, anyway. I'd just have to deal with the pain for a few weeks, and live with a tailbone that was not only facing inward, but now also tilting a bit to the left.

That's okay; I thought to myself, *the rest of me isn't quite right, either.*

A CONCUSSION AND A BROKEN FOOT

It never failed. Every time my husband would leave for a few days, bad things would suddenly start to happen. It was like God was up there looking down saying, "Oooh! He just left the house again; let's see if she can handle this one!"

My husband was deployed to Iraq, and was gone for almost a year and a half total, with only a two-week break in the middle of his deployment. Of course, that was the year when everything in our home decided to break down, our family dog died, the snow was deep as could be, and the worst injury to one of our children had occurred.

Our son was at school one day, playing dodge ball, when he collided with another student. They somehow smashed their feet together, and then he fell and hit his head on the floor.

As a result, our son received injuries to both his foot and his head, and wasn't acting right at all. His friends had seen the incident, noticed his odd behavior soon afterward, and decided to bring him to the school nurse to be checked for injuries. She called me about the incident and I quickly drove to the school to check on him.

When I arrived, I ran to the nurse's office. As soon as I saw my son, I knew something was wrong. He didn't look well at all, and was talking in a very strange and confusing

114

manner. An emergency room visit was now obviously necessary.

I had the school quickly gather my other children from their classes, so they wouldn't arrive home after school to an empty home. Then I headed outside to the car with my injured child, who absolutely refused to be wheeled out of school in a wheelchair. He stubbornly hopped out on his good foot instead.

On the way to the emergency room, he still wasn't making much sense when he was talking. I was getting more and more worried as he started complaining of severe head and foot pain.

I started to drive a little faster, not realizing I was now over the legal speed limit. Of course, I was stopped for speeding. I explained to the officer what had happened and where we were going.

After taking one look at my son, he realized the seriousness of the problem. He was very sympathetic to our situation and told us we could be on our way, but gave me a strict warning to slow down as I drove to the emergency room.

The kids thought this was very amusing and talked about how mad their father would be if he knew I'd just been pulled over for speeding. I didn't find it amusing one bit, and was growing more and more concerned with my son's situation. He was still not looking very well at all.

A few minutes later, we arrived at the emergency room. After a very long wait, a few tests, and a full examination, the doctor finally gave us his diagnosis: a broken foot and a concussion.

By this time, our son was starting to talk a little more clearly. Even though he was still in a lot of pain and was exhausted from the events of the day, he was now starting to find the entire situation funny as hell. I guess watching Mom go into panic mode over his injuries and then get pulled over for speeding, was very amusing!

A few days later, we were able to go to a follow-up appointment to get a cast placed on his broken foot. It was the very first appointment they had available to do it.

At the doctor's office, they put a cast on both his foot and lower leg. He found the entire process fascinating, but was already annoyed by the itchiness that had settled in by the time we left the office.

On the way home from our appointment, he asked if we could take a little detour to the pet store, just to look around.

Feeling a bit sympathetic to his situation, and knowing he was now going to have to deal with walking around on crutches for a while, I figured, *Why not?*

And that is where we found Wallace.

CHAPTER ELEVEN

PETS

WALLACE

While at the pet store, our son, who was still recovering from his recent injuries and now sporting his brand-new cast and crutches, told me it would help him feel much better, and recover a whole lot quicker, if he was allowed to get a pet rat.

I knew he was giving me a line of BS so he could get the rat he'd been wanting, but at that point I'd had enough for one week and simply gave in.

Now, I know a lot of people would squirm in their seats at the mere thought of a rat, but they truly are wonderful pets; and some of them have great personalities, as well. It's kind of like having an ugly, oversized guinea pig.

As we started looking at the ones on display, without hesitation he picked out an extra-large, black-and-white male rat. The store clerk took it out of the cage and handed it to him.

I took one look at him, snuggling nose-to-nose with this huge rat—which also seemed to be enjoying the attention—and quickly decided I was making the right choice. They looked perfect for each other.

We purchased the rat, and a few items to go along with him, and headed for home.

As we drove home, we thought of several names for the rat. By the time we reached home, our son had ultimately decided on Wallace as a name. It suited him well.

By that afternoon, our other two children had also arrived home from school. They noticed the new rat as soon as they walked through the door, and couldn't wait to start playing with him.

It was nice seeing them excited about something again. Between the recent emergency room trip for my son's broken foot and concussion, and the deployment that my husband was still away on, it had been a rough year so far.

That night we received a call from my husband—a video chat on the computer. It had been a couple of weeks since we'd heard from him, so he didn't know about the injuries our son had recently suffered or about the new pet rat we'd recently adopted, so as I ran to answer the call, I told the kids to sit quietly in the background for a minute, so we could surprise him with the new rat.

We started our conversation that night with the usual questions. After a few minutes had gone by, I slowly turned the camera to our son, who now had a huge grin on his face. His broken foot was propped up on a chair and his new pet rat was ever-so-casually perched on top of his cast.

My husband noticed the cast and the rat right away. As a look of disbelief washed over his face, he asked, "What happened?" and "Is that a rat?"

As he tried to process what he was seeing on his computer screen, I started to laugh. All three children jumped in on the conversation and started to tell their father about the exciting day they'd had, riding to the emergency room…and how Mom got pulled over for speeding…and how we got a cool new pet rat named Wallace. They were so excited to be able to share their news with their father.

He sat quietly, listening to their stories for a while. As his look of disbelief started to fade, a smile slowly replaced it. I couldn't believe it—he usually protested any time we tried to bring a new pet into our home, but this time, he just had to laugh.

Apparently, having him deployed thousands of miles away, with a recently injured child, was the best way to get him to agree to one. *Hmmm,* I thought. *I wonder how many other pets we can get while he's away.*

The answer, as it turned out, is one cat and one dog.

End of Discussion

Now, to understand why my husband would typically protest any new pets coming into our home, I should explain just how many pets we've had over the years, and how some of those pets ended up in our home to begin with.

A lot of them were rescues, some were rehab patients found injured on the side of the road, and others…well, let's just say he didn't have much say in them coming to our home at all.

Our son was the proud owner of a playful tiger cat, which he absolutely loved. This cat was well taken care of and adored by all of us, but now our daughter wanted a cat of her own to take care of as well.

I figured, *Why not? It'll teach her about responsibility and give our other cat some company when the kids aren't playing with him.*

I asked my husband if he was okay with us getting a second cat. His response was, "We're not getting another cat—end of discussion!"

I'd merely asked him one, simple question, and I sure as hell didn't think it required that kind of response.

So…in reaction to that wonderful response from my husband, I brought our daughter to our local animal shelter and adopted a new cat. The cat had a new home, our daughter was happy, our other cat had a companion to keep him company throughout the day, and the best part of all…my husband learned it was *not* a good idea to try to tell his wife what she could and could not do.

Of course, that decision completely backfired on me later on, as we soon realized just how snooty of a personality that cat actually had. She had what I liked to call the "I'm the queen and you are my servant" complex. Not what we would have hoped for in a pet. And, of course, whenever she had one of those moments—my husband will always comment, "Real great job picking that one out!" Ugh.

Don't Mess With the Bird

Inside our home, the pecking order has always been a little backward. Before our bird died of old age, it was: bird beats cat; cat gets mad and beats dog; dog crouches and hides behind people; people see bird flying toward them and run like hell. That's just the way it was.

Our pet bird—a cockatiel at the time—would chase our other pets, and occasionally, a person or two around our home whenever he was let out of his cage. That is, he'd do that before he went blind.

Yes, we had a blind cockatiel. He lived to be twenty-three-and-a-half years old. For some crazy reason, our pets don't like to head toward that light.

He was a sweet little bird, but unfortunately, I was the only one who could handle him. He'd bite everyone in the family but me to let them all know that he was the one in charge.

He'd chase the cats and the dogs, nip at their paws and tails, and even jump on their backs as they tried to run away. It was his favorite game to play.

One cat, which we still have today, used to swat at him with his paw. He also thought it was a fun game to play.

Our dog, a Siberian husky at the time, was the only one who'd truly fight back with this bird. If he caught her just right, she'd start to growl and snap back at him, so we had to watch them closely whenever he was out of his cage.

Once the bird went blind, he stayed in his cage, and the cat was then in charge.

BOBBER

Our oldest cat, Bobber, is now the one in charge…at least he thinks he is, anyway. We adopted him from our local animal shelter back in 2004.

What a great companion for our child. He's a white cat with a few spots of orange on him. He was around three years old when we adopted him.

We chose the name Bobber for him because the child who is the proud owner of this cat loves to fish, and after watching this cat go from being still for hours to suddenly jumping up and down and darting all over the place, that name seemed very appropriate.

One of our other children thought it would be funny to shorten that name a bit, and now calls him Boob, so now he answers to that name as well.

He's a playful cat and has a great personality, but also has a bit of an attitude. He just loves to get in trouble and hear people yelling his name. He's done so many different, crazy things that he should have his own chapter in this book. On any given day in our home, his name is being yelled at least once or twice throughout the day, in phrases like:

"Bobber! No!"

"Bobber! Get out of there!"

"Bobber! Stop playing in the dog's water!"

"Bobber! Get off the counter!"

"Bobber! Leave the poor dog alone!"

"Bobber! Damn it! Somebody get me the squirt bottle!"

"Where's that cat now?"

He's always getting into trouble, or at the very least, he's in the way, as he has to be a part of everything everyone is doing at all times. He's not an ordinary cat. He's our Bobber, our Boob, and he's definitely the one in charge.

Soon after we adopted him, he decided he didn't like the idea of the bird being in charge. He started doing everything he could to put him in his place.

We noticed he'd play with the bird by reaching through the bars on the cage and bopping him on the head with his paws. I guess that's how he was getting even with him for all those times when the bird attacked him when he was out of his cage.

One day, years before our bird went blind, I decided to let him out of his cage so he could stretch his wings a bit. He started flying around the house and above the stairs that led to the lower level of our home.

The cat saw his opportunity and, without hesitating, leaped into the air after the bird. His front legs were stretched out as far as he could get them to go. He looked just like a flying squirrel in mid-flight as he suddenly disappeared into the stairway.

We then heard a loud thump as the cat and the bird both slammed into the wall at the same time. He'd caught the bird in mid-flight.

I ran toward both of them as fast as I could to check for injuries. Both were a bit shaken, but okay. I then placed the bird back into his cage and scolded the cat, who was now looking a bit insulted.

A few minutes later, I saw the cat sitting near the birdcage. He was once again reaching through the bars, trying to swat the bird in the head. He doesn't like to lose, and as usual, he just had to get the last hit in.

Oh, but it doesn't end there...

Bobber the Peacekeeper: Anytime our two dogs would get too rowdy when they started to play, our cat Bobber decided this wasn't allowed. He would run after both of them, hissing and smacking them with both front paws. Our dogs—an oversized Labrador retriever and full-grown German shepherd—then ran away in fear when they heard this little cat starting to hiss, growl, and run after them. They ought to know that the cat doesn't like them running around making noise in the house. Sheesh.

Bobber the Disciplinarian: I was working on something in the kitchen one morning when I suddenly heard our son, who was around eight years old at the time, start to scream as he ran down the hallway toward me. I ran over to see what the problem was. This cat was hissing and spitting as he chased him down the hallway, mad as hell. Apparently, our son had done something he didn't like, and he was going to teach him a lesson. I had to get between the two of them so I could protect my child from this pissed-off cat. Boy, was he mad!

Bobber the Center of Attention: Typing on the computer is also not allowed in our home when this cat wants attention. When we try to type, he'll either walk in front of the computer monitor so we can't see it, or he'll lie down on part of the keyboard so we can't type. If we try to ignore him, he'll lie down directly on the mouse, so we can't use that, either. If we try to move him, he'll bite our hands and then run like hell.

He'll also chase and attack the cursor as it moves along the computer screen, if he's feeling playful enough.

If none of this works to get our attention, he'll walk back and forth in front of the screen until he's noticed and given the proper attention. If we still try to ignore him, hoping he'll just stop and go away, he'll walk across the desk, sit down, stare at us for a minute or so, and then touch our face continuously with his paw until we acknowledge him.

We finally had to provide him with his own basket to sleep in, so he can be next to us while we work on the computer. This was the only thing, besides continuously tossing him off the desk, that would keep him from walking in front the screen. And if we didn't grab him just right when tossing him off the desk, we were often bitten, because, as it turns out, touching him in any way other than petting is not allowed.

A little side note here: As I was writing this very story, trying to type on my computer, Bobber stopped to pat me on the head and walk in front of me yet again. He apparently wanted to make sure I got his story right.

Bobber in the Bathroom: This cat loves fresh water. I don't mean he likes to have a bowl of fresh, clean water given to him daily—I mean he likes to drink it straight from the tap.

Bobber comes into my bathroom every morning, jumps up on the countertop, and rubs his face against the faucet handle until I turn it on for him. He's even turned on the water by himself while doing this.

I then turn it on for him, and he pushes his face against the faucet to turn it back off. I then turn it back on for him again. Of course, he turns it back off again.

Then I raise my voice, tell him to stop, and warn him that it's his last chance to get a drink of water. Then he finally leans in and drinks the water as it slowly runs out of the faucet.

After that, he sits down to watch me finish getting ready for the day, now satisfied that he's once again made me go through the little ritual of turning on and off the faucet three times before he gets his drink.

I've tried kicking him out of the bathroom on several occasions, as I'm starting to get tired of this little routine of his, but as I said before, pushing him off of any surface can get us bitten. Besides that, it doesn't matter how many times we kick him out of the bathroom—the only way to keep him out is to close the door. Then he'll sit outside and cry while pawing at the door to try to get back in.

Bobber and the Bubbles: Another way he gets his water is to wait for me to give the dogs their fresh water. Then he plays with any bubbles that have formed from the force of the water being poured into the bowl. He'll sit and paw at the bubbles floating around, then he'll lick the water off his paws.

If there are no bubbles to play with, he'll pat the water with his paw until he makes his own. Our dogs will actually sit and wait until he's done playing before he allows them to get their drink of water.

When he's done playing, he walks all over the house, leaving wet, little paw prints on the floor. I finally purchased a rug to place next to the water bowl so he'd have to dry his feet as he walked away from the bowl, but of course, he jumps around that rug to avoid it.

He just loves to hear his name being yelled as he walks away, leaving a long trail of paw prints behind him. Whenever we try to clean out the dogs' water bowl by emptying it completely, so we can wipe it out, if we don't refill it with clean water quickly enough, he'll jump into the bowl with all four feet until we yell at him to get out.

Bedtime for Bobber: Soon after everyone goes to bed, Bobber starts to meow very loudly, sometimes while carrying a fabric toy ball in his mouth. He walks all around the house while doing this, until someone answers him or walks out to get him for the night.

When no one responds, he'll choose the nearest bedroom door, walk in, jump on the bed, lie on top of the person in bed, and reach out and touch them in the face with his paw for attention—not a pleasant thing to wake up to, when he's just finished playing in the dogs' water.

Blessed by Bobber: Any time anyone in our household sneezes, our cat Bobber gives a meow in response. He'll do this even while he's sleeping, although that meow is typically a bit quieter. We don't know if he's irritated by the noise, or just simply trying to say, "God bless you."

Bobber the Bugslayer: During the summer months, when everyone is going in and out of our home, we occasionally get a few flying insects that find their way inside. When this happens, Bobber is in charge of taking care of these bugs. He'll chase any little insect he can find in our home until he's caught, killed, and eaten it.

He's jumped up to five feet in the air, trying to catch these insects. And if he can't reach them by jumping, he'll sit on the floor and make funny meowing noises until someone picks him up so he can catch them with his two front paws. It's a little gross to watch him eating these bugs, but it's also nice having an automatic bug-catcher in our home at all times.

Bobber at Christmas: Every holiday season, we bring a Christmas tree into our home for decorating. When this is done, Bobber climbs into the tree and tries to knock it down. He's done this more than once, so he knows he can do it, and continues to try it again and again with each new tree. What he doesn't realize is that we now tie the tree to the wall every year. Let's see him try to figure that one out.

Bobber last Christmas: This past holiday season, we chose to put up a fake Christmas tree. Oh, how my husband was thrilled with that decision. No more getting stuck with needles, dragging an oversized tree up a steep hill, and lifting the tree up over our heads to tie it to a vehicle smaller than the tree itself. And no more tying it to the wall in our house to avoid having it knocked over by the cat.

But between the problems of an injured arm on the child who usually helped drag the tree up the hill, and crazy college schedules that didn't allow time for the entire family to go out together, for the first time in years, we gave up on the idea of getting a real tree and dug out the fake one instead.

We missed the pine smell and the usual fun that came with getting the tree, but it still looked beautiful. We were hoping the cat wouldn't be interested in the fake one that year.

Unfortunately, the opposite occurred. This fake tree evidently piqued our cat's curiosity. It became a daily challenge for him to ruin as much as possible in and around the tree. Apparently, he didn't like this kind of tree, either.

Every day we found him trying to knock an ornament out of the tree, chewing on the lights, or messing up the tree skirt and nativity scene underneath it.

For some silly reason, he seemed to have a personal vendetta against the Virgin Mary statue in the nativity scene. She was knocked down every morning. Several other mornings, the entire nativity scene was in complete ruins.

What he had against the nativity scene and the Virgin Mary, we'll never know.

One morning, I woke up and caught him in the act. He was still under the tree and still at it—running around like he was high on drugs. The nativity scene was in ruins once again, the tree skirt was all balled up in a mess a few feet away from the tree, and a large ball of red, white, and green string had been unraveled, leaving a trail of string from one room to another.

This was the part that was not a normal daily occurrence. The ball of string was something our son had made for Christmas one year. It was used as garland on our tree. It was long enough to cover more than two extra-large Christmas trees, so whenever we used it to decorate our tree, we'd leave the extra leftover portion of it, still balled up, at the base of the tree. We'd push it securely into the branches at the bottom of the tree, out of sight, so the cat wouldn't be able to pull it out and play with it—or so we thought, anyway. But that morning, Bobber had been determined to destroy as much as possible, and somehow managed to get it loose.

He'd had a lot of fun with that ball of string, and had it almost entirely unrolled. It went around the base of the tree several times before the rest of it headed out toward the kitchen, about twenty feet away. There was string everywhere, and he was still running around after it.

I immediately grabbed the squirt bottle, which was now being stored within a few feet of the Christmas tree, and went after him. He saw the bottle in my hand and ran for cover so fast that I didn't even get a chance to squirt him.

After all the years of trying to discipline this cat whenever he was doing something wrong, he'd learned to run like hell whenever he saw anyone with the squirt bottle coming in his direction.

I needed a new weapon. He wasn't intimidated by any of us anymore, and I swear he was laughing as he ran for cover!

A few minutes later, I was still working on cleaning up the mess he'd created when I heard him start meowing. It was that sad kind of meow that I'd always heard from him right before he'd throw up.

I ran over to make sure he wasn't on any rug-covered surfaces, just in time to see him barf. I looked down at the mess, and was instantly agitated by what I saw. There were parts of the Christmas tree in the barf. Of course—I should have known he had to taste this one, too.

I cleaned up the smelly barf mess first, and then finished cleaning up the remainder of his destruction.

As I finished cleaning up, I noticed something: no ornaments were on the floor that morning! Yay! He must not have gotten to that yet.

Half an hour later, he was up the tree once more, trying to knock the ornaments down. Ugh. I wonder if the stores sell an extra-prickly, cat-proof Christmas trees?

Bobber Wants Out: We installed a cat door inside the main door that leads to our cellar, so our cats could get through the door anytime they needed to use the litter boxes we set up for them downstairs. Bobber doesn't like having to maneuver through this cat door, so he gets through the door a different way.

We have a set of bells that were hung on the doorknob of our cellar door years ago. One day, Bobber decided to start playing with them to see what would happen.

What happened was, someone opened the door for him.

Now, whenever he wants to get through the door, he paws at the bells until someone hears the noise and opens the door for him. He'll do this for a long time, as he's very stubborn and likes to get his way. After listening to those bells jingling for a few minutes, most of us would simply give in and open the door.

At first it was kind of cute; but not so much anymore.

After being awakened for a second time two nights in a row, listening to this cat paw at the bells for what seemed like forever, I decided the next day I was going to make him use the cat door, like he was supposed to be doing in the first place. I know it would have been easier just to remove the

133

bells from the doorknob, but I wanted to see whether I could teach him that he couldn't use the bells to get through the door again.

The next morning I had my opportunity. He started with his usual pawing at the bells, waiting for his door service. This time, instead of opening the door for him, I tapped on the cat door instead.

This seemed to have him confused. He had to think about it for a few seconds, but then I heard him paw at the bells once more. So I tapped on the cat door again. He pawed at the bells again. This went on and on, with us going back and forth, for about five minute or so before I finally heard him let out a soft meow. He was obviously confused. Why wasn't anyone opening the door for him? He was pawing at the bells, as usual.

As we'd been doing this, I'd been watching him through the cat door. It was made of clear plastic, so I could see him easily. He was looking all around, not understanding why the door wasn't being opened for him, and he didn't see me watching him through the cat door.

Then he turned around and noticed me peeking in at him. He wasn't happy. He stuck his paw through the cat door at me, meowed, and then went back to pawing at the bells, more determined than ever. He wanted me to open the big-people door for him, so he could walk through it like everyone else, and he was not happy with what I was doing.

He pawed at the bells again, and I tapped on the cat door once more in response. I refused to give in on this one, so after another minute, he finally gave up and maneuvered himself through the cat door with a look of disgust on his face. He wasn't happy he'd lost that battle. Apparently, in his mind anyway, I'd forgotten that he was the one in charge, not me!

He still paws at the bells every now and then, hoping someone will open the door for him. But when I hear him do this, I just tap back on the cat door to remind him that I'm not his personal door person. After a while, he gives up and walks through the cat door, but almost always with a look of disgust on his face.

Bobber in Flight: Our son's friends, all teenagers at the time, decided they wanted to get together for a fun night of playing board games and cards. Since they were all staying late into the night, they decided to camp out in our living room, where they'd be the most comfortable.

As one of them slept on the couch that night, Bobber was watching from the second-floor loft area above. At 5:00 in the morning, this guest woke up to see Bobber staring down at them. Bobber seemed to be having a staring contest with him. He obviously didn't like this new person sleeping on the couch that he customarily slept on.

Just as our guest was pointing out our cat's strange behavior to a few of the others in the room, Bobber jumped from the second-floor area to the couch down below, trying to land on top of him. Completely startled, the guest reacted by catching the cat and throwing him back into the air.

The other guests watched in amazement as Bobber landed with a thud against the door. That instantly woke everyone else in the room.

Bobber wasn't happy, but he was okay, and he'd made his point—that he was still the one in charge. After that, he merely walked off. The kids all slept with one eye open for the rest of the night.

During another overnight stay, this time in our basement, one of our guests was sleeping on the floor and woke up to find Bobber touching his face with his paws. Apparently, he'd been watching him sleep and wanted to check him out.

Immediately recognizing that this was the same cat that had previously jumped on top of their friend from one floor above, this guest slowly and carefully reached up to pet him and say, "Nice kitty." Evidently, Bobber appreciated this. He got up and simply walked away. I guess this guest met with his approval.

Bobber the Protector: Our family was relaxing on our back deck one night, when all of a sudden our German shepherd decided it was time to play. She started jumping on me and biting me in the arm in her usual manner. She does this often, and is usually very careful not to bite too hard when she's playing, but if we aren't careful or quick enough, she can catch us just right and do some real damage.

I was definitely not quick enough that day, and being startled by what she'd just done, I let out a scream of surprise. At that, Bobber, who'd recently become a bit protective of me, decided he wasn't going to allow that behavior from our dog. Without warning, he jumped off the chair he was sitting on—yes, he has to have his own chair on the deck with us, because he thinks he's a person, and not a kitty—and attacked our dog by biting, swatting, and hissing at her.

The dog turned her attention from me to the cat and started to defend herself by trying to stomp on him. Bobber started to fight back. We now had an absolute brawl on our hands.

The entire family jumped in to help break them up. We didn't know who was going to win the battle, but we sure knew it wasn't going to end well.

Somehow, I think the cat would have won, but at least the dog finally got in a few good hits that day.

That's our Bobber—our Boob—and our largest source of both frustration and daily entertainment.

Just a small update: Bobber passed away just before this book was published. He is greatly missed. Rest in peace, Bobber—we miss you...and for heaven's sake, be nice to God! He's the one in charge, not you!

SQUIRREL!

We've always had several bird feeders hanging on a post in our backyard. Because of this, we see all kinds of wildlife activity. This can include a wide variety of birds, squirrels, chipmunks, turkeys, and even the occasional raccoon or deer.

On most days we can walk into our home and see the cat or dog—or sometimes both—sitting and staring out our windows, waiting for this wildlife to come into our yard.

On one particularly nice, sunny day, our dog—a slightly overweight black Labrador—and our cat Bobber were both intently looking out the tall, glass window in our back door. The cat was making an excited, broken-up kind of meowing noise and shaking his tail like crazy. The dog was also shaking her tail and was starting to drool on the floor. I quietly walked over to the door to look out the window and see what the excitement was all about.

It was a large, gray squirrel, dangling upside down with a mouthful of birdseed in both cheeks.

Ugh! I thought. *Not another squirrel! There goes the rest of my birdseed!*

If that darned squirrel stayed there any longer, I wasn't only going to lose the last of my birdseed, but both the cat and the dog were going to have heart attacks from the excitement of it all.

I thought to myself, *What would be the worst thing that would happen if I opened the door and let the dog out after this squirrel? My dog will get some much-needed exercise trying to chase the squirrel, the squirrel would be scared and might never return to my bird feeder again, and the cat will have some entertainment, right?*

It seemed like a win-win situation, so I stepped in front of the cat, gently pushed him out of the way, and opened the door for the dog.

To my surprise—and the squirrel's surprise as well—not only did the dog take off running, but the cat did too.

Oh shit! Didn't expect that! He'd scooted around my legs and shot out the door before I could catch him.

The squirrel instantly jumped down and ran at full speed toward the tree line, which was about three hundred feet out back. I couldn't believe it. The squirrel was barely keeping ahead of them, and the dog and the cat were going the exact same speed.

I've never seen that fat, old dog run so fast before, I mused. *And look at that cat run!* He was determined to get that squirrel, which was half his size! What a sight it was, watching our dog and cat both chasing a squirrel together, at the exact same speed.

They all made it to the tree line within seconds. The squirrel darted up the nearest tree, within inches of both the dog and the cat that were now at the base of the tree, trying to figure out how to get to him.

I ran out to grab them. They both protested wildly as I tried to carry the cat and drag the dog by the collar back to the house at the same time.

I sustained a few scratches along the way, but I did manage to get them both back to the house in one trip. Wow, was that a struggle and a half.

As I reached the house, I walked back in and shut the door behind me. Both the dog and the cat rushed back to the door to try to get back outside.

The squirrel was still watching us from the top of the tree. He stayed there for a few minutes before he decided to make a move.

Not what I expected when I first opened that door, but it had definitely solved the problem. After that day, we never saw the squirrel or any of his little buddies at our bird feeder ever again.

Problem solved.

A PENNY SAVED

It was just another day. We'd started it by running errands. As my daughter and I got into the car that day, I noticed a penny lying there on the car seat. I picked it up and said to her, "Find a penny, pick it up; then all day long you'll have good luck." She giggled in response.

We were soon on our way. As we finished running our errands that day, I decided to make one last stop at a pet store to see if we could find toys for our dog and cat. They were both at home, feeling very depressed from the recent loss of our other dog and cat, who'd both died earlier that year of old age.

As we walked toward the toy section, we saw a few cats that were on display from a local pet shelter. We noticed that one of them looked very similar to a cat we'd had years ago. She looked adorable.

Our daughter immediately started with the usual begging. "Can we get her?"

Without skipping a beat, I reacted with my usual response: "Absolutely not. We have too many animals already, and I don't want any more to take care of after you kids have all left for college."

Then we noticed the age of the cat printed on the tag on the front of the cage. They figured she was between five and seven years old. *Oh, shoot!* I told myself. *Here it comes.*

"But Mom, this one is an older cat!" The previous argument I'd just used was now a little less relevant, since the cat would probably not be living past the time our youngest left for college, anyway.

After much debate and thinking about the poor, depressed, and lonely pets we already had at home, I figured this might essentially be a great companion for our other cat, and maybe even the dog, too.

I told her if she could somehow convince her father to agree to the adoption, we could get the cat. I figured there was no way he'd agree to get another animal anyway, so that would be the end of it.

She then called my husband from the pet store while he was out on a snowboarding trip with our son. After only a few minutes of pleading, he actually agreed to the adoption. I couldn't believe it. *Since when does he agree to get more cats?* I wondered. *Ugh!*

"Okay, but this is the absolute last animal we adopt!" I told her.

We then filled out the paperwork and made plans to pick up the cat a few days later, after the paperwork had been approved.

As we drove home, we tried to think of the perfect name for our new cat, but after all the names we'd chosen for all the animals we'd adopted over the years, there didn't seem to be any good ones left.

As soon as we arrived home, I noticed another penny lying on the floor in our kitchen.

Wow, another penny! That's weird—that's two today!

Later that evening, my husband and our son arrived home from their snowboarding trip and started to tell us all about their trip that day and how much fun they'd had snowboarding, and how they'd even found a penny that day.

Okay, now that is really weird, I thought. *What is with all the pennies today?*

At that point, our daughter spoke up and said, "Hey, why don't we name the cat Penny? We found all these pennies today, so it must be fate—she has to be named Penny."

We all agreed that was a good name. The cat was then officially named Penny.

Over the next two days, we were finding pennies all over the place—in the driveway, on the floors at grocery stores, on sidewalks, and around the house.

Unbelievable! I've never found so many pennies in all my life.

We received the phone call a few days later stating the paperwork had gone through for the adoption, so we drove back to the store to pick up the cat and bring her home. She was a sweet and lovable cat who was extremely scared by her new surroundings, but was steadily adapting a little bit each day.

After that day, the pennies stopped randomly appearing. Now we were finding little pee spots everywhere instead. The cat was apparently so nervous from the stress of being adopted that she'd started peeing everywhere but the litter box.

Ugh! I continued to clean and throw away almost everything the cat had peed on. After much work, some pet relaxation products, and a lot of love, the cat finally started using the litter box.

A couple of years later, our family went through some changes and this cat's favorite person left for college. This caused Penny to become stressed out all over again, resulting in the same peeing issued we'd had before.

By then, I'd had it. I decided it was time to have a talk with our daughter about giving the cat to someone with a more stable environment. She protested like crazy, of course.

Over the next couple of days, we started finding pennies everywhere. We took that as a sign that we were supposed to keep the cat, so we tried to work through her stress issues once more.

I cleaned and threw out a few more things and confined her to our master bedroom and bathroom area, giving her a litter box, food, and water dish all her own.

After a few weeks of being confined to that one area of our home, she finally started to relax. She adjusted well and started to consider our bedroom area as her safety zone. Thankfully, she went back to using her litter box. It was a lot of work, but at least for now, no more pee spots.

I guess the saying should go a little more like this:

"Find a Penny, pick it up, and all day long…well…you'll have to clean up pee."

And I thought potty training the boys was bad. Ugh!

ADOPTING AVA

Our newest dog, Ava, is quite an interesting dog. This is the story of how we ended up with her:

We had a Siberian husky years ago who was absolutely beautiful. She was all white, with two different colored eyes, and had a great personality. After she died of old age, our family was extremely sad over losing this dog. Our other dog that was left behind, the black Labrador, then became very depressed and lonely. She wasn't eating very well, and was slowly starting to lose weight.

Hoping she'd come out of her depression on her own, and not wanting to deal with another dog right away, we decided to wait it out for a few months, to see whether she'd get any better on her own.

Over the next few months, the dog improved, but was still not the same, so we decided it was time to get a new dog. My husband was adamant that he was going to be the one to choose the new dog this time. He decided a German shepherd was the breed he wanted next. We both agreed that it had to be at least two years old, so we could avoid the nasty chewing-and-peeing phase that typically come along with new puppies.

We started our search, and after finding several dogs that weren't quite right for our family, we decided it was time to try our luck once again at our local animal shelter.

As we walked through the sea of barking dogs, we could barely hear each other as we commented on each one we saw.

When we finally reached the back corner of the shelter, we noticed a sweet-looking, two-year-old German shepherd shivering in the corner of a very small cage. She was so skinny that her ribs were showing, and she could barely fit inside the cage she was being kept in.

She was obviously scared by her surroundings and was so happy to see us standing there. She tried desperately to lick our hands through the cage.

We could tell right away that she was a sweet, lovable dog, in much need of a good home. The children all started pointing to her as my husband looked over in our direction. They'd made their decision—they wanted that one.

He took a brief look at the dog and we all walked out to the front desk to finish our discussion where it was much quieter, away from all the other barking dogs.

Once we arrived at the front desk, we started asking the receptionist a few questions about the dog we'd just seen. She was the perfect age—two years old—so we hoped there'd be no chewing and peeing to deal with. Since she'd seemed like a sweet and lovable dog, we decide to adopt her right away.

My husband looked confused. "Did _we_ decide to get that one already?" he asked.

It was funny—he didn't remember making a decision on that specific dog.

As he looked at our kids, he knew he wasn't going to have much choice. "Okay, she seemed sweet enough, we can get her," he told them.

As we filled out the paperwork, we were told she had to be spayed and checked by a local veterinarian before we could pick her up, so we finished the paperwork and headed for home without her.

The dog was sent to a local veterinarian, who informed the animal shelter, who then informed us—after we'd officially adopted the dog, of course—that she was only one year old, not two.

This wasn't something we wanted to hear. *Oh well,* we decided. *She's ours now. Maybe the chewing and peeing phase we were trying to avoid won't be too bad.*

A few days later, we received a call that the dog was ready to go home. So we gathered the kids and went to pick her up from the shelter.

Upon arriving home, our other dog, Maggie, the black Labrador, was happy to see a new dog coming into the house, but she was also very cautiously checking her out.

Our new dog walked right past her, into our home, and immediately started pooping on the floor.

Well, so much for being old enough to avoid the potty-training phase.

We briefly scolded her and then brought her outside to finish her business, where we then praised her like crazy. Thankfully, this little accident only happened the one time. She was a smart dog and a quick learner. We were thrilled to have her.

After much discussion, we finally came up with a name: Ava. What a sweet dog.

The next few weeks went something like this:

I came home from work one day to find Ava had chewed and completely destroyed my sneakers. *So much for avoiding the chewing phase.*

No big deal, I thought. *They were ready to be thrown out anyway.*

I then went to the pet store and purchased a few chew toys for both dogs, hoping to curb our little problem. They were both thrilled with the new toys and were now chewing them constantly.

Maggie was now starting to come out of her depression. She was enjoying her new companion very much. They'd play together all the time—and boy, did Ava have a lot of energy. She was definitely still in that high-energy puppy stage.

The next day, she chewed and destroyed Maggie's favorite toy. Now Maggie was once again acting very depressed, and started to protect her toys. Every now and again, we'd hear her growl if Ava was too close to her toy.

I purchased a few more toys, similar to the one that had been destroyed, so there wouldn't be any more problems with sharing. The dogs then started to share all of them, and Maggie was now happy once again.

A few days later, we decided it was time to purchase new dog beds for the dogs. The ones we purchased were a little expensive, but they matched our furniture perfectly. The dogs, without question, loved them.

The very next day, I came home from work to find that Ava had chewed up both new dog beds. My husband came home from work that day, saw the mess, and was downright furious. He'd already had it with our new dog and her destructive behavior, and was now blaming me for picking out the wrong dog at the animal shelter. After all, he didn't pick this one out—we did.

The next day, I arrived home from work to find that Ava had now chewed up part of my favorite wooden bench. She'd left teeth marks in the wood and wood shavings all over the floor.

I scolded her once more and sent her off to her room. Yes, she now was being punished with time-outs in her room—something we still do with her to this day, whenever she gets into trouble.

Obviously this dog didn't like it when we left her at home alone. She was chewing everything in sight, every time we left. We decided to leave both dogs locked up in the garage over the next few days, so nothing else would be destroyed while we were at work for the day.

On one of those days, I gave both dogs some comfortable, old blankets to sleep on and a few chew toys to play with while we were gone.

After work, I arrived home to find that Ava had chewed my boots that were out in the garage with them. To top it all off, parts of my boots were now lying on top of the now-shredded blankets that I'd given them earlier that morning.

That's okay; I can deal with this too, I thought to myself. *The blankets were old, and I was looking for a reason to buy a better pair of winter boots anyway.*

After that little incident, we took all of our footwear out of the garage and started to place them inside closets and lockers instead.

Over the next few weeks, Ava continued to chew on any blankets I'd given them to sleep on, and any shoes that were within reach

At that point, I was forced to try a new approach. This time, I placed an extra-large, decorative basket on the floor and filled it with all the dogs' toys. That way, they could get whatever toys they wanted, whenever they wanted them.

I then placed a few stuffed animals that the kids no longer wanted into the basket, along with a few new chew bones I'd purchased for them.

I showed both dogs where their basket of toys was and encouraged them to take them out any time they wanted one. I figured this way I could teach both dogs that those toys were the only items they were allowed to chew on.

I then replaced the torn blankets they'd been lying on with some small throw rugs, and prayed my efforts wouldn't be in vain this time.

It worked. She finally stopped chewing on our shoes, and they now both enjoy playing with the toys from the basket. They also now enjoy sleeping on the new throw rugs I gave them.

Of course, getting them to pick up their toys and put them back into the basket is a whole different matter. We're still working on that.

SCREEN-DOOR GREETING

One summer, as we stood on our back deck talking with a friend who'd stopped by for a visit, our dog Ava came running over to our back door to see who our new visitor was. She started whining as loud as she could as she tried to figure out how to get to us through the screen door.

We tried to talk to her to calm her down, but it wasn't working. She'd already noticed our new visitor and just had to come check him out to make sure he was okay.

Not wanting to have her licking and jumping all over our new guest, we left her inside, behind the door, figuring she'd calm down after a few minutes on her own.

She wasn't happy with this, and decided she was going to get outside any way she could. So how did she accomplish this? Well, she simply went through the door on her own. Yes, our German shepherd, as stubborn and strong as she now was, pushed her way through the screen door, knocking it completely off its frame and onto the ground. She then ran over to our new guest. Once he was fully inspected, she casually walked off and started playing in the yard.

What a greeting. We all stood there in complete shock at what she'd just done. It took me a minute, but then I shook my head and laughed as I introduced our new dog to our guest.

I guess the cat isn't the only protective animal in the house, after all.

ᎧᏗCHAPTER TWELVE℘Ꮶ

Simple Tasks vs. Everyday Life

The stories in this chapter are a little bit longer than some of the others in this book. The reason for this—simple tasks aren't always that simple.

I Only Wanted a New Pair of Boots

After our dog Ava chewed up my winter boots, I decided it was time to start shopping for a new pair. *Not a problem,* I thought. *I'll just grab a new pair the next time I go to the store. No problem at all.*

Wow! I couldn't have been more wrong!

I started by checking out the boot section of every store I stopped in. Unfortunately, none of them had anything good in my size. After a few weeks of having no luck finding anything at all, I decided it was time to try another approach.

In early November, the winter weather was now well on its way. I ordered a new pair of boots online from a well-known, reputable company and received the boots in the mail a couple of weeks later.

I quickly realized they'd sent me the wrong size, so I mailed them back and asked for a replacement pair in the correct size. One month later, I still hadn't received my boots, so I called the company to find out what was going on with my order. The boots were now out of stock for that size, so they had to credit the money back to my account.

It took two months and another phone call before this company refunded my money, and that was after they'd put an urgent request on my refund and sent it to the refund department—which, I was told, no longer took calls. *Really? Ugh!*

Next I visited a local store that I hadn't checked out before. There I found three styles of boots that would all be good enough, but of course, the store didn't have any in my size.

I then went back online. After searching through several web sites, I finally found one that had a pair in my size and in stock. It was a company I hadn't ordered from before, but I decided to take a chance, since they had good consumer reviews.

What could possibly go wrong this time? I thought to myself.

I placed my order, and shortly after, received an e-mail confirming the order. Yay! I'd soon have a good pair of boots. The e-mail said they'd arrive in only a few days.

Two weeks later, nothing had come in, and my credit card was never charged, so I e-mailed the company to ask where my order was. Days later, still nothing, so I called them.

They told me they were still working on their holiday orders—my order had been placed January first—and they were going to call me back with a status.

Four days later, still no phone call, so I called them back again. The woman who answered the phone told me she'd find out what had happened to my order and promised to call me right back.

Two hours later, still nothing, so I called them back again. They were now telling me that the lady that handled those orders was having trouble with her furnace and hadn't come in yet, and they'd try to get in touch with her and then call me right back.

Wow! I asked myself. *Can it really be this hard to talk to someone regarding my order? I only want one, lousy pair of boots! Why is this so difficult?*

One hour later, a lady from that company called me back regarding my order. I couldn't believe it—someone actually returned my phone call. Wow!

She told me their company was going through an upgrade at the time I placed my order, and even though I'd received an e-mail confirmation, they'd never received the order. She said she'd check on the availability of the boots I wanted and then call me right back.

Two hours later, still no call, so I called them back again. A different woman answered the phone this time and told me the lady I'd previously talked to was now out to lunch. She'd have her call me right back as soon as she returned from her lunch break.

Yeah, right! I thought. *I've heard that one way too many times already. I'll just plan on calling them back in an hour.*

A half hour went by and the phone rang. This woman actually called me back. *Wow! I'm impressed!* I thought. *They have one employee who follows through on phone calls.*

But of course, it wasn't good news. They'd misplaced the one set of boots they thought they had left in my size, and when they found the box, it was marked with the wrong size.

Bottom line: they no longer had any boots left in my size. So I cancelled my order. They apologized for the confusion and said they'd send me a $25 gift card for all my troubles. *Okay, I guess that's fair. Ugh!*

Once again feeling defeated in my quest for new boots, I headed back to the stores. Once again, there was still nothing in my size.

I refused to give up at this point. *This can't be it!* I thought. *I have to have boots for the winter—the snow is already on the ground.*

I looked around on every shelf in every store, and finally found a store that had one nice pair of boots that was made by a well-known company. They were full price and one size too big, but would fit well enough if I wore an extra pair of extra-thick socks along with them. Quite frankly, wearing sneakers in the snow was not working out very well, so I decided to go ahead and purchase the boots.

As I carried them toward the front of the store, I found three other items to purchase along the way. I walked over to the cashier with all four items in hand. After I was done cashing out, the cashier handed me the receipt and I read it over. I couldn't believe what I was seeing—he'd charged me twice for the boots!

I went back and showed him the mistake, and he told me he couldn't fix the problem, but the customer service department would so he then sent me there to deal with the issue.

As I walked over to the customer service desk, I had several questions running through my head: *Why is this so difficult? Why can't I just go to a store like a normal person, pick out one, lousy pair of boots, and simply purchase them, like everyone else? Why? I only wanted one, lousy pair of boots! Why is this so difficult?*

Once I reached the customer service desk, I showed my receipt to the woman behind the desk while I explained the error. She looked it over and told me she'd credit the overcharge back to my account right away.

Okay—not a problem, I thought. *At least I'll get my money back.* By then, I was just glad that my new boot-purchasing nightmare was finally over—or so I thought, anyway.

I finally have new boots...Yay! That night, I wore the boots outside for the very first time. I was so glad to have a pair of boots for the winter. The snow was now piled high, and it was absolutely freezing outside. They were a little big, but worked out great by keeping my feet dry and warm. *What a nice pair of good boots,* I thought to myself.

The next day, our daughter borrowed them to go outside. A few minutes later, she came back inside with a piece of boot in her hand, saying the tab on the string had broken off—the one that holds the top of the boot in place against the leg, so the snow won't get in.

That figures! I fumed. *I'm so glad I paid full price— not once, but twice—for these so-called quality, brand-name boots!*

I placed the tab on the string and tied it back in place to temporarily solve the problem.

I then checked my account statement to see whether the credit had ever been issued for the overcharge at the store where I'd purchased them. Of course, it wasn't. So I called and explained the problem to the lady who answered the phone.

She, of course, had no idea why the refund hadn't been issued yet, and gave the phone to her manager. The manager then told me that with some banks, it may take anywhere from three to ten days to see the credit. I thanked her for her time and made a note to check my account again in a few days.

A few days later, I checked my account once more. The credit had finally been refunded. I was so glad that little issue was taken care of. *Could my boot-purchasing nightmare now actually be over?*

Well, not quite. I still had the matter of the broken tab to deal with.

The third time I wore my boots, I put them on and pulled on the tab to tighten the top portion against my leg. The tab immediately fell off into my hand.

I then tied the tab back in place once again and wore the boots outside in the snow, hoping it would stay in place. Once I was back inside, I pulled on the tab to loosen the boots, and it fell off in to my hand once more.

That was it—I'd had it! I cursed at my new boots and every person and company I'd dealt with over the prior months. Then I threw them off into the corner. I took a deep breath, gathered myself together, and tried to figure out what to do next.

I wasn't returning those damn boots! I'd gone through too much already, and couldn't deal with one more person in customer service.

I gathered up the boots once more and tried to figure out how to fix the problem. I tied ridiculously large knots on the ends of each string to help keep the tabs in place. It didn't look very good, but I figured that would help fix the problem.

What a cheap pair of boots! I threw them off to the side yet again and walked into the kitchen, mumbling to myself.

My husband had heard the commotion and asked what the problem was. I told him it was time to move some place warmer where there was no more snow to deal with and no more need for any winter boots!

Seeing my miserable mood, he quickly agreed, and then headed in the opposite direction.

After another two weeks went by. I never received the $25 gift card from the last online order I'd tried to place. Oh well—I didn't want their lousy gift card anyway.

I then checked my statement once again for my refund from the first online order I'd made months ago, when I'd had to return them because I received the wrong size, and still nothing.

That's the last time I order anything from them! Not wanting to deal with another phone call, I decided to wait a few more days before I called to complain again.

Another two days went by and I received a check in the mail. It wasn't the direct refund to my account, like they'd said it would be, but a check was just fine with me! *Could it be?* I wondered. *Is my boot purchasing nightmare finally over?*

I couldn't believe it. I was actually done with the oh-so-simple task of purchasing one, lousy pair of boots.

Oh, how I hate my overpriced, cheaply made, extra-large, twice-paid-for, crappy new boots! We're moving south for the winter.

THE TREADMILL

It was time to buy a treadmill. Yes, it was once again time for the usual routine of shopping around and doing months of online research before we made what should have been a simple purchase.

Several times, we'd chosen a model that would have done well, but each time, my husband had refused to spend the amount of money the stores were asking for them.

Finally, the day arrived. We'd done our research, chosen a model that we liked, and knew of a local store that was having a sale on that specific one.

Upon arriving at the store, we not only found the model we'd chosen, but two other models that were also good as well. They'd been marked down to a clearance price and had an extra twenty-five percent off as well, because they were now selling the floor models.

I couldn't believe what I was seeing. This was my chance to end all the running around, once and for all. I had to convince my husband that this was the best deal he was going to find on one of those things, and I had to do it quickly, before he changed his mind.

A few minutes later, he was talking to two different salesmen, asking them several questions about each of the treadmills on display. Then he tried one of them out.

After comparing two of the models side-by-side, he actually found one he liked. He asked me if it was the same brand we'd thought was so good when we'd done the research with our son the week before. I told him I wasn't sure, but would text our son to see if he could verify it for us.

Within minutes, our son texted back.

Yes it is.

That did it. We'd finally found a treadmill he was willing to purchase. No more running around, comparing prices, and doing research. Yay!

Now it was time to pay for the treadmill. My husband started with the usual questions for the salesman, trying to get as many more discounts as he possibly could. As usual, the salesman just laughed and said no, because we'd already gotten the best possible deal on it.

Then we learned the store wanted to charge us $180 to deliver and set it up.

I couldn't believe it, and neither could my husband. He quickly decided we'd do it ourselves.

Now we had to make the decision as to whether we wanted the extended warranty that came with it. After much debate, we finally chose a plan. My husband handed the cashier two coupons that allowed $10 off any purchase of $50 or more.

There's no way she's going to take both coupons, I thought to myself. But I stood quietly by, waiting to see how he was going to try to make this one work.

The cashier told him she couldn't take both coupons on one purchase. He responded, "Yes, but we're purchasing two different items—a treadmill and an extended warranty for the treadmill."

I started to laugh. Nice try, but of course this didn't work; she only accepted one of the coupons.

We finished our transaction and headed for home.

Once we arrived home, I walked inside to thank my son for sending the text that had helped us make the final decision to make the purchase.

As I explained it to him, "Your father never would've made that purchase if you hadn't sent that text message saying it was a good brand to buy."

He started laughing and said, "Oh yeah, about that...I was getting in the shower at the time, and just gave you a quick answer. I don't really remember if that was the brand we researched or not."

Visions of my husband doing more research and possibly wanting to return the treadmill suddenly started to swirl through my head. I could see by the expression on my son's face that he was envisioning the same scenario.

We quickly agreed to never tell his father, and we never spoke of it again.

About two days later, we went back to the store to pick up our new treadmill. A couple of hours after that, we had it parked in our driveway and were trying to figure out how to get it into our basement. Somehow, it had looked smaller in the store.

I then looked at all the men in our family, who just couldn't wait to try it out. Oh, the excitement of it all! The testosterone was really flowing now.

The treadmill was already assembled, because it had been a floor model, so all we had to do was carry it down a flight of stairs, set it in place, and plug it in. Easy…right?

Wrong. Nothing is ever that simple with our family.

My husband and our oldest son started rolling the treadmill off the trailer and toward the stairs that lead to our basement. Thank God, that heavy thing had wheels.

But now they looked confused. How were they going to get that heavy piece of equipment down the stairs and through such a narrow door?

They stood around, contemplating how they were going to make it work. After a few minutes, our son decided he was going to take measurements to make sure it would fit before they tried to move it any further.

He walked to the bottom of the stairs, measured the doorframe, and then yelled up the stairs, "No problem—it'll fit."

He added, "We just need to put it through the door at an angle, and it should fit just fine."

Okay, here we go.…

166

My husband got one end of the treadmill, as our son and I both grabbed the other end, and all three of us carefully walked it down, one step at a time.

As we tried to maneuver together down each step with this large piece of extremely heavy equipment, our son kept stepping on my feet. There just wasn't enough room on the steps for all four of our feet.

This had me yelling each time I was stepped on, and him laughing as he tried to avoid my toes. *Of all the days to have worn flip-flops! Ugh!* Sneakers would have been so much better that day.

We finally arrived at the bottom of the steps, and then we noticed a problem: the treadmill was just not going to fit, no matter how much we angled it.

I watched as the two of them tried it several different ways. It just wasn't going to work. They stood there, holding the treadmill in place. It was now leaning halfway through the door, entirely blocking it.

I suggested taking the door off its frame to make more room. "That might give us just enough room to angle it through," I told them.

My husband wasn't happy, but he agreed to try it. And since the treadmill was now blocking the doorway, I had to run inside the house and down the other set of cellar stairs to hold his side of the treadmill, so he could find something to remove the door with.

As my son and I both stood there, holding the treadmill in place so it wouldn't fall and get damaged, my husband retrieved a battery-powered screwdriver from the workbench.

As he walked away from us, we heard him start muttering something about how he should have done the measuring himself. I thought about making a comment, but decided to bite my lip and hold it in instead.

No sense in poking the bear, I thought to myself.

He then walked back over and started unscrewing the hinges, but was having trouble reaching a few of the screws, because we were standing in the way of the door.

He managed to work around us somehow, and the screws started to come out just fine. One after the other, they started falling to the floor as the doorframe loosened its tight grip on the wall.

As he started unscrewing the very last one, the head of the screw started to shred and he could no longer get a good grip on it. He then examined the screw and immediately started to curse. It was just not going to come out using that screwdriver.

Oh no! I thought. *I'll never be able to hold my end of the treadmill long enough for him to solve that little problem!*

At that very moment, our son, who was still holding the other end of the treadmill at a somewhat awkward angle, must have noticed me struggling. He decided he'd be more effective if he was on my side of the treadmill, holding it with me. So he ran into the house, down the other set of cellar stairs, and around to my side to help.

Once he had a firm grip on the treadmill, I took a quick break from holding it and ran to retrieve a flashlight and a few more screwdrivers for my husband to try. Then I ran back over to the treadmill to help my son continue holding it in place.

In the meantime, my husband was trying every type of screwdriver we had, but none of them worked.

We were starting to laugh at this point—we just didn't know what else to do. The treadmill was getting heavier and heavier, and the last screw was not coming out.

At this point, our son was starting to sweat profusely and I was getting tired and sore. As we stood there side by side, trying to hold the treadmill in place, I was trying my best not to touch the sweat that was now starting to drip down his forehead and arms.

It didn't work. He tried to adjust the way he was standing against the treadmill and his sweaty arm touched mine.

"Ewww, that's gross!" I yelled. He thought that was funny, since I couldn't move to wipe it off, and started to laugh hysterically in response.

Oh, for the love of God, please hurry with that last screw! I thought.

After a few more minutes had passed, my husband finally found a screwdriver that was working. *Yay! It shouldn't be much longer,* I thought to myself.

He started to move the screw in the right direction, and had it over halfway out, when it suddenly started to shred once again.

I just couldn't help myself—I started to scream, "No! Are you kidding me?"

He then started to swear even louder and walked back to the bench to look for more tools.

My son and I were now both laughing hysterically at the entire situation we'd gotten ourselves into. We had a brand-new treadmill stuck in the doorway that we could barely hold onto, it now had a few scuffmarks on it, and we were all battered, bruised, and sweating from all the effort of trying to move it and then hold it in place. My husband was now swearing like crazy, and we were now going to have to put our cellar door back together when we were all done.

Oh, why didn't we just pay to have it delivered and set up? I groaned inwardly. *It would've been so much easier!*

As for my husband, he was retrieving yet another tool to try to fix our little screw problem. While he was doing this, my son laughingly suggested that I should try to reach up and see if I could get the screw the rest of the way out myself, using my hand.

It only had a little way to go, and we were now getting desperate, so I figured it couldn't hurt to try. I reached over and grabbed the screw and instantly started to scream—it was burning hot, and I'd just scorched my fingers on it.

Why would I do such a stupid thing? I knew my husband had just tried to get it out using an electric screwdriver, and it was obviously going to be hot at that point from the friction.

Just another blonde moment, I guess. My oldest was now laughing so hard he was having trouble holding up his end of the treadmill. Smart aleck. I don't know who he gets that from!

Now my fingers were burning, my son was dripping sweat and laughing hysterically, and my husband was absolutely throwing a fit because he couldn't get the last screw out. To top it all off, his brand-new treadmill was getting all scuffed up while we continued to try to hold it in place.

About a minute or so later, my husband walked back over with a hammer and a crowbar in hand, determined to get the door off its frame. As I saw him walking over with that look of determination on his face, I quickly ducked my head down and started praying that both the screw and the door wouldn't come flying off in our direction.

He placed the crowbar against the screw and slammed the hammer into the crowbar, breaking the screw in half. Then he grabbed the door as it fell off its frame.

Yay! That part was finally over and we were all still alive. Woo Hoo!

Now it was time to try fitting the treadmill through the doorway again.

I stepped out of the way and watched as they maneuvered it several different ways. It still wouldn't fit. *It's so close! Ugh! Now what are we going to do?*

I looked at the doorframe and the treadmill once more, and then cautiously suggested to my husband that it might be time to try taking the doorframe itself apart.

He wasn't happy. That was going to take forever to put back together, but we didn't have much choice, so he decided to try it.

He unscrewed the doorframe—no problems with those screws that time, thank God—and then they both tried to slide the doorframe around the treadmill.

As they were doing this, they asked me to run around the other side to help. I heard them both laughing as they told me to hurry.

As I darted up the stairs, I knew they were just messing with me, but by then, I was just happy to be running away from the situation.

By the time I reached the other side, they'd gotten it through, already had it in place, and were now standing there, smiling at me as I walked through the doorway.

Once the treadmill was in place they stopped and looked it over thoroughly. They both had a look of concern on their faces.

"What's the matter?" I asked. Then it hit me—there was no key to turn it on.

"Where's the key?" I asked.

They looked at each other once more and then my husband asked, "They never gave it to us at the store, did they?"

"Ugh! Are you kidding me?" I said. "How could they forget to give you the key? And how could you both leave without it?"

Unbelievable! After all that work, we weren't even going to be able to try it out!

My husband then called the store and talked to the person who'd helped them load the treadmill onto our trailer. The man apologized, saying he'd forgotten to give it to them. He said he had both the key and the manual at the store, and would hold onto it for them until they were able to return.

By this time it was now 9:00 p.m. and we were all exhausted—and we still had to reassemble the doorframe. So we all agreed it would be best to pick up the key and manual the next morning.

Since my husband and I were both busy the next morning, our son drove to the store to pick up the last few things for our treadmill. Once he was back home, he put in the key and tried it out.

He'd only run on it for about ten minutes when the machine shut off on its own. He couldn't believe it.

He did a quick inspection and couldn't figure out what the problem was. He still had the key in place, and it was still plugged in.

As this was happening, my husband was texting him, asking how it was going with the new treadmill. There was no way our son was texting his father back to tell him there was another issue with the treadmill—not after what we'd just gone through with it the night before!

He never did get an answer to his text until about an hour later, when I arrived home and we figured out what the problem was—a fuse had blown. The treadmill had been plugged into the same outlet as a dehumidifier that had been running at the same time, and it was just too much for the fuse.

We fixed our little fuse problem, plugged the machine back in to a different outlet, and it worked just fine—thank God!

Our new treadmill had a few, small scuff marks on it, like the rest of us did after our little adventure getting it down the stairs and through the cellar door, but we got a great deal on it, saved $180 on a delivery and setup fee, and it was working just fine. And the best part...it was finally over. Yay!

As I sit here, trying to type in my office, one floor above, I now hear the sounds of slamming feet as our son runs on our new treadmill downstairs. As he's doing this, lights are flickering above us with each step he takes.

I guess we'll need to place some padding underneath it to help with the noise, and then find a powerful outlet to plug it into, so the lights don't continue to flicker.

Of course, our cats both had something to say about the new treadmill, as well. Bobber slept on it a few times, to check it out, leaving white little kitty hairs all over it and Penny was so stressed out from the sheer size of it that she decided to pee on it.

Maybe we should just give up on the treadmill idea and go back to walking outside instead.

CHAPTER THIRTEEN

LAUNDRY

THE REJECT PILE

It was a typical day—go to work, run errands, chauffeur the kids from one place to another, and then grab some quick leftovers for dinner. It had been a long week, and we hadn't had a good meal in days.

Since I had the next day off from work, I figured it would be the perfect day to make a nice, home-cooked meal for our family. That night, I told my family if they chose something from the freezer and took it out so it would be thawed in time, I'd make a nice meal with it the following night.

I was tired and heading to bed extra early that night, so they agreed to make a decision on the following night's dinner and finish cleaning up for the night.

I started the dishwasher, put a few things away, picked up a few stray pieces of clothing, washed up, and then headed for bed.

The next morning I woke up and took my time getting dressed and ready for the day. It was nice to have a morning where I didn't have to rush. Just as the last person ran out the door, I headed toward the kitchen to start my day.

As I walked in, I noticed the sink and countertop were overflowing with dirty dishes. It's amazing how many dirty dishes can accumulate within a twelve-hour period when there are three teenagers living in a home—they're like eating machines!

I looked around for the dinner that was supposed to be thawing out overnight, and discovered that nothing had been taken out. That figures...they never remember to do anything unless I ask ten times, or write a reminder note and stick it to their foreheads.

Oh well, I thought. *I guess it's just another quick, out-of-the-box kind of dinner for tonight. So much for a nice, home-cooked meal.*

I looked around and found some pasta I thought would do nicely. It wasn't going to be a nice roast or ham, but at least I could prepare some fresh vegetables to go with it.

As I turned around to place the pasta on the counter, I realized there wasn't any room left to place anything. *Okay,* I sighed inwardly. *I guess it's just going to be one of those days.*

The next hour or so went a little something like this:

I opened the dishwasher to start filling it with dirty dishes, only to discover that the dishwasher had been run the night before—by me—but never emptied.

So I emptied it, filled it with dirty dishes, added dishwasher detergent, and pressed the Start button once again. Then I pried a sticky jar lid off the countertop that had been left there overnight and soaked it, along with the jar it went to, in some soapy water.

Then I tried to throw something away, but found the garbage can overflowing. I had to take that outside and then replace the bag. Then I started to clean the countertops, so I could have a clean place to prepare dinner, and found myself wasting time scrubbing the spot where the top of the sticky jar lid had been stuck.

Then I rinsed out the sticky jar and lid that had been soaking and tried to recycle it, only to find that the recycling bin in the kitchen also needed to be emptied.

I tried to empty that into a larger recyclable bucket we'd stored in our cellar, and quickly realized that it also needed to be emptied. So I emptied that bucket and prepared a bag of recyclables for garbage day.

While I was doing that, I noticed the cats' food dish was empty. So I filled it with food and then finally returned to the kitchen, where I'd originally started. Whew!

Now, I thought to myself, *maybe I can actually start preparing dinner.*

I washed my hands, and as I grabbed the hand towel to dry them, I realized it was time to replace it with a clean one, so I took the dirty one into the laundry room. That's where I discovered an extra-large pile of laundry, still waiting to be done.

I hadn't done laundry in two days, and of course, no one else had bothered to do any, either. It was really starting to pile up now. So I gathered all the remaining laundry from every laundry basket in the house—all full, of course—and then dumped them all into a pile on the floor in our laundry room.

I looked at the pile I'd just created, and knew it was going to be a full day of doing laundry once again—it was massive.

I let out a sigh of exasperation and then dug in. I separated the clothes by load type, but refused to check the pockets. I'd already warned my family that if they wanted me to continue washing their clothes, the least they could do is check their own pockets and place everything right-side-out.

As I was sorting through the mountain of laundry that stood there before me, I noticed that quite a few items were still inside-out and all bunched up. To top it all off, one pair of pants had something hidden in the pockets once again.

That was it—that was my breaking point.

What am I, the maid? I fumed. *Sheesh! There are four other people in this house that are all perfectly capable of picking up after themselves and doing everything I've already done this morning, yet they couldn't bother to take dinner out of the freezer, start one load of laundry, feed the cats, empty a dishwasher, the garbage can, or the recycling bin, or properly prepare their own laundry for me to wash for them?*

Ugh! I absolutely refused to stick my hand into one more dirty sock to make it right-side-out before washing what could have been washed by the person who'd worn it in the first place. *I haven't even had breakfast yet!*

I decided, right then and there, I'd had enough that morning. That's when the Reject Pile of laundry first appeared.

I took all the clothing that had something left in the pockets or was still bunched up and inside out, and threw it into a pile on the floor in the hallway next to our laundry room.

I then filled the washing machine to capacity with some of the remaining clothes, added detergent, and hit the Start button.

After all that was done, I returned to the kitchen, sat down, and ate my breakfast.

The rest of my day consisted of my regular day-off routine of making dinner, doing chores, cleaning up, picking up, and catching up.

The rest of my family all returned home later that afternoon and immediately noticed the clothes on the floor as they walked in. They wanted to know why their clothes were lying in a pile on the floor like that, and why we were having plain, old vegetables and pasta again for dinner.

I told them I'd explain everything during dinner. They all walked away, shaking their heads in disgust and confusion.

That night, as we sat and ate our wonderful meal together, I took my time describing all the things I'd done that morning. Then I went on to clarify how my new laundry Reject Pile System was going to work.

I ever-so-casually explained to all of them that, if they didn't have their laundry properly prepared—pockets empty and clothes right-side-out—they were going to end up in the Reject Pile until they fixed the problem. And if they didn't like it, they could start doing their own laundry from now on.

Everyone quietly shook their heads in agreement and then finished their meal without a word.

After that day, I enjoyed a few weeks of my family cleaning up after themselves and helping out with the housework. They even did a few loads of laundry that week. And the best part is that now, when I do laundry, all the clothes are right-side-out and almost every pocket is empty.

I wish I'd thought to do that years ago. It worked great! Now if I can only get them to remember to take out dinner the night before.

LOAD OF SHAME

After I'd been a parent for a while I quickly learned to separate my laundry into several different piles—whites, colors, darks, delicates, and those really disgusting items that need to be rinsed before they even touch any other article of clothing. In our house, we call that pile the Load of Shame.

The Load of Shame evolved one day after I found several articles of clothing, covered in mud and sweat, mixed in with our regular dirty laundry. This was the type of dirty clothing that makes me cringe when I see it touching my clothing in the hamper.

It wasn't the first time I'd found something disgusting mixed in with my everyday laundry. And to top it all off, it was mid-summer, with high temperatures, and it had been sitting at the bottom of the hamper for more than two days before I'd discovered it.

182

I now have a separate, small hamper for the Load of Shame. When anyone has any clothing that qualifies, I tell them to add it to the Load of Shame basket so I can rinse it with hot water before washing it with our other clothes.

Now I just wish I could figure out how to place those disgusting items into the washing machine without actually touching them. *Yuck!*

Check Your Pockets

It was another typical day. I gathered up the dirty laundry from all the laundry baskets, separated clothing by load type, and didn't bother to check the pockets. I then ran the first load of wash. When it was done, I threw it into the dryer.

A little later, when the dryer was finished, I opened the door and started pulling out the clothes to start folding them. As I did this, I noticed a pair of jeans with a pocket that was inside out, so I placed my hand inside the pocket to push it back in place. As I did this, I noticed something sticking to my fingers, deep inside the pocket.

Oh no! I thought. *I don't want to know what I just stuck my hand into!*

I slowly pulled my hand out of the pocket and discovered the gum that had been left inside. *Gross!* I immediately washed my hands and then set the jeans aside to deal with later that day.

My daughter—the proud owner of those gum-filled jeans—arrived home from school later that afternoon. As I described the mess I'd found in her pocket that day, I reminded her once more about checking her pockets before placing anything into the laundry. Then I suggested she place the jeans into the freezer to harden the gum. I'd heard that freezing gum made it easier to remove it from fabric. We hoped it would help to save the jeans.

She headed off toward the kitchen with her jeans in hand, but instead of placing the jeans directly into the freezer, she decided to squeeze and play with the gum first, to try loosening it from the fabric. After doing this for a minute or so, she gave up and finally placed them into the freezer.

Our son arrived home from school later that afternoon, went into the kitchen, discovered the jeans in the freezer, and asked me why I was now placing clothes in the freezer. Had I completely lost my mind? My husband heard our conversation and was now wondering the same thing.

"It was to freeze the gum that was stuck inside the pocket—I swear!" I insisted.

Later that night, my daughter took her jeans out of the freezer to see whether the gum would come off, but it still wasn't working. She now wanted to know why freezing the gum hadn't worked.

"Gee—I don't know," I retorted. "Maybe because you squeezed the gum into the jeans several times before placing them into the freezer!"

She looked at the gum and poked and prodded it for a few more minutes before finally giving up. Next thing I knew, she had a pair of scissors in her hand and proceeded to cut a huge hole in the pocket to remove the gum. Patience wasn't a virtue she possessed, in that instance. I guess there won't ever be gum in that pocket again.

STILL GOOD

Time for another load of laundry. I gathered up all the dirty laundry from around our home, separated clothing by load type, and once again refused to check the pockets. I started a load of wash and continued with my other household chores for the day.

Later, when I heard the timer go off on the washing machine, I opened it up and found our son's cell phone inside, on top of the pile of laundry. It was filled with water and completely destroyed.

I took it out and tried to see whether I could get it to work, but it wouldn't even turn on. I set it aside to explain what happened later on.

Children can be pretty difficult to live with when they lose their phones for a while. Our son went through cell-phone withdrawal symptoms for a week, as we refused to spend money on a new one. We decided this would be a good time to teach him about responsibility and reinforcing the check-your-pockets rule before placing any dirty laundry into the baskets to be washed.

After a week had passed, my husband thought it would be a good idea to replace the cell phone with an older one we'd set aside that no one had been using. It was a much older cell phone that had been replaced years prior, but we knew it would still work once we had it charged, so he made the trip to the cell phone company and had them reprogram the old phone.

Once he arrived back home, he gave it to our son, who was very excited to have a working cell phone again—he didn't care how old it was! As my husband handed him the cell phone, we reiterated the rules about checking his pants pockets before placing them into the laundry basket.

We also explained that, if he wasn't careful with that cell phone, he was going to have to pay for the next one. We refused to pay for something he'd been so careless with. This was his absolute-last chance, and he had to be careful with it!

Our son was so excited! He was going to be extra careful and check his pockets every single day—he promised!

"Okay—here you go," my husband said as he handed it to him.

A working cell phone—yay! He couldn't wait to start using it.

He opened it up to check it out, and then immediately dropped it to the floor. The battery went one way and the rest of the cell phone went the other way. My husband and I looked at each other and then back at our son, who was standing there with a look of shock and panic on his face.

We couldn't believe it! He'd only had the cell phone in his hands for a second, and it was already in pieces on the floor.

He picked up the cell phone, shoved the battery back in, and quickly checked to see if it was okay.

As he darted out of the room with the cell phone in hand, we heard him yell out, "Still good!"

How to Save an iPod

This same child, when he was thirteen, left his iPod in his jeans pocket. I still refused to check the pockets of each piece of laundry; consequently, both jeans and iPod were thrown in the wash.

Later that day, I opened the washing machine and found his iPod and earphones wet and twisted inside. I could see the moisture that had built up inside the screen of the iPod, and knew it wasn't going to work.

I gave it back to him later that afternoon and gave another lecture on why he should always check his pockets before placing his dirty clothes into the wash. No big deal, according to him—he had an idea.

He'd heard from one of his friends that he could save an iPod by simply placing it into a bowl of rice. The rice would absorb the moisture and save the iPod, he told me.

I agreed to the experiment, in hopes of saving the iPod, and pulled out an extra-large container of rice from our pantry. I handed it to our son, who opened it up, dropped in the iPod, and started to shake.

My husband and I looked at each other in amazement. We were absolutely dumbfounded at what he'd just done.

I guess I should have specified that I meant to have him pour a little bit of rice into a small bowl to place the iPod in; not throw the iPod into the entire gallon-sized container of rice we'd planned on eating over the next few months.

Lesson learned...be more specific before handing over an entire supply of rice to a child.

By the way, the rice trick did work. Truly amazing!

PICK UP YOUR CLOTHES — LAST WARNING!

Busy, busy, busy—that's family life. Parents work, kids go to school, and the afternoons usually involve running errands, making dinner, doing laundry and dishes, cleaning up, and driving back and forth, to and from after-school activities.

On one of these typical days of running around trying to keep up with everything, I started picking up the house and doing a bit of cleaning while I had a few minutes to spare.

As I was doing this, I noticed what was quickly becoming an ongoing problem—dirty clothes lying on the floor beside the hamper in our son's bedroom. Not only were there clothes on the floor inside his bedroom, but there were even more clothes lying on the floor outside his bedroom.

I'd told him several times before to pick up his clothes, and had even placed a laundry basket in his room for him to use.

This was unacceptable. He was now reaching adult age, and I'd grown tired of picking up after him.

I stuck my head inside the door and told him to pick up the clothes immediately, and to start using his hamper from now on.

"This is your last warning!" I announced.

After about an hour or so, I noticed the clothes were still lying on the floor.

Okay, I thought, *obviously this isn't working very well.* I wasn't going to tell him yet again to do something he should have done already.

This time, I decided to try a different approach. I gathered up all the dirty clothes on the floor outside his bedroom and walked outside into the backyard. I then walked about three hundred feet, until I reached the tree line—yes, it's a rather large backyard—and found a tree with very high branches. I proceeded to throw every item of dirty clothing into the highest branches of the tree.

By this time, our other children had gathered at the back window and were now watching what I was doing. They were laughing hysterically as they watched me throw the clothes into the tree.

Our son was still in his bedroom, unaware of what I was doing. By the time I walked back into our house, the two kids who were standing at the window laughing had now quieted down and were cautiously staying out of my way.

I then walked back into our son's bedroom and informed him of the whereabouts of his clothes. I told him if he wanted them back, he was going to have to climb up a tree to get them.

He came out of his bedroom with a look of confusion and disbelief on his face and walked to the back door. I then stood there with my other two children and watched as he walked all the way out back and climbed up the tree to retrieve his clothes.

As he worked his way up each branch, trying to rescue every piece of clothing, I grabbed my cell phone and started taking pictures so I could forward them to my husband at work. His coworkers found them hysterical.

Our other two children watched and laughed as their brother started to throw his clothing to the ground. He then climbed back down the tree with a look of disgust and embarrassment on his face, gathered the remaining clothes off the ground, and brought them back into the house to place them in the hamper, where I'd asked him to place them in the first place.

A little extreme? Well, maybe. But I made my point, the problem was solved, and now all three children place their dirty clothes into their hampers without me asking.

ℭℎapter Fourteen

Oops and Ewwws!

IN A MEETING

As most college students know, doing well on final exams is an integral part of achieving a good overall grade point average. When most kids receive high marks on their exams, they're usually very excited about it. Our kids are no different.

One day, our daughter had taken her final exams at college and had just gotten the news that she'd received a ninety-seven on the one she was most worried about. It had been one of her most difficult classes.

She was so excited. She texted both my husband and me right away, saying:

<u>I got a 97 on my final exam!</u>

For months, my husband's cell phone had been randomly sending text messages to people in his contact list.

Soon after he received this text from her, she received one of those random text messages back from him.

The message simply said:

<u>In a meeting.</u>

What? Are you kidding me? She couldn't believe what he'd just done.

She immediately texted him back, saying:

<u>You can spare five seconds to tell me you're 'in a meeting' but you can't say good job? What the hell, Dad?</u>

Totally confused by the text he'd just received from her, he checked his phone message history and figured out what had happened.

After explaining it to her, they both found it hysterical.

Now, whenever she texts with a good grade or any other good news, he makes sure to respond with:

<u>Good job!</u>

Or the occasional

<u>In a meeting</u>

Just to agitate.

LUNCH VIDEO

One day our son, who was around four years old at the time, had been playing nicely throughout most of the day. As a reward for his good behavior, I told him he could watch a video while we ate our lunch together.

He found one of his favorites, popped it into the VCR player—yes, it was a long time ago—and started watching it as I prepared some sandwiches.

A few minutes into our lunch, I'd already finished my sandwich, so I walked out of the room to start working on something else, leaving him to finish his lunch and watch the rest of his video.

Soon after I left the room, he apparently decided he was done watching the video and took the tape out of the VCR player. Sometime during that moment, curiosity must have kicked in about the inside workings of the VCR player, because once the tape came out, his sandwich was the next thing to go in.

He pushed it in as far as it would go, and then quickly realized it wasn't going to fit the rest of the way in on its own.

So what did he do next? He retrieved a tall broom and used the handle of that broom to shove the rest of the sandwich into the VCR player.

I returned to the room just in time to see the last of the sandwich being shoved in. Why, oh why, would anyone do that? There's no way I was going to be able to fix that.

The inside of the VCR player was damaged by the broom handle and there was peanut butter and jelly everywhere. It was all over him, the rug, the broom handle, and had completely covered the VCR player inside and out. Oh, he was so lucky he was still little and cute.

I had to purchase a new VCR player, along with a new locking mechanism for it. We also had to give our son a lecture on how sandwiches were not made for VCR players.

As for me...well, I learned never to leave that child alone with a sandwich and a VCR player ever again!

ICED TEA AND GREEN OLIVES

One night, after having just sat down to relax a bit before bed, I heard my son (around twelve years old at the time) in the kitchen, grabbing yet another late-night snack. He'd gathered up an extra-large glass of iced tea and a small bowl of green olives to take downstairs to his room. This was one of his favorite snacks, and since a late-night raid on the kitchen was a normal occurrence in our house with our growing kids, I wasn't paying much attention to what he was doing.

As he started his descent down the stairway, I suddenly heard him yell. Then I heard a loud crash, a splash, and a glass tumbling down the stairs. I jumped up to see what had happened. Evidently, he'd tripped over the toy soldiers he'd been playing with on the stairs earlier that day. He'd fallen and spilled both the bowl of olives and the iced tea. They were everywhere.

I just had to laugh. He was looking up at me with a look of disbelief and was absolutely covered in iced tea and olives. Thankfully, he wasn't hurt, but what a sticky mess. It was all over the place—on the stairs, on the rug at the top of the stairs, on the banister, the walls, and all over him as well.

It looked like the toy soldiers had been fighting him off, using olives and iced tea, and our son had totally lost the battle.

The only question I had was, "Why is it that you wait until I'm finally sitting down to relax for the night to make the biggest mess possible?"

His response was a look of confusion, mixed with a little bit of disgust. I think he was expecting me to ask, "Are you okay?"

THE PROJECTILE VOMIT CURSE

All right, so normal children vomit when they're extremely sick...I've got it. But what causes a small child to projectile vomit every time they throw up? We have one son that did this until he was almost two years old.

And when I say projectile vomit, I mean he was known for it. People would be hit from up to ten feet away. If he was in bed at the time, he'd not only cover himself and his crib, but also his toys, the wall, the dresser, the floor, and anything else that happened to be within range. What a mess it was, every single time.

That sound a child makes just before they throw up wasn't something we ever wanted to hear coming out of his bedroom at 3:00 in the morning. There was nothing worse than being awakened in the middle of the night to the sounds of this child projectile vomiting.

We'd run into the room to help—usually in bare feet and in the dark, of course,—only to be greeted by a slippery mess and a few, very small, extra-sharp, barf-covered objects that had been left out on the floor. We always managed to step on those, somehow. And that would occasionally result in a few screams as well as a few choice words. This, undoubtedly, is how our son learned to curse.

IT'S HOVER OR COVER

As we all know, public restrooms can be extremely disgusting at times, but to most young children, they seem to be just another place to go pee. They don't understand at that young age just how unsanitary some of those places can be.

While out on one of those horribly long shopping trips one day, I had to use the restroom. As usual, almost every stall I saw that day had something unmentionably gross in it, on it, or around it.

197

Knowing I wasn't going to make it home at that point, I knew I was going to have to use one of those atrocities So, I chose the least-offensive one. Being a protective mother with a very young child at the time, I had my daughter come into the stall with me and told her not to touch anything as I tried to do the same.

For privacy reasons, I'd always tell my children, "Watch the door for me, and make sure no one comes in." That usually kept them looking the other way, giving me the privacy I needed. It also made them feel like they had an important job to do as well.

On this day, however, after watching the door for what seemed like only seconds, my daughter suddenly turned around and asked me why I wasn't sitting down. Then she proceeded to give me a little push so that I would.

That, of course, knocked me off balance. Not wanting to land on the floor, I chose the toilet seat instead.

At that very moment, my inner voice sounded a little something like this: *Oh, gross! Oh my God! What did I just sit in? Eeewwww! I didn't want to touch that! Son of a b—— ! Now what do I do? Where's my hand sanitizer? Shoot! Did I bring it with me? Where is it? Oooohhhh myyyy God! Where is it? Grooooss! I so need a shower! Eeewwww!*

I then finished up in the bathroom and immediately headed for home. As I drove home, I had a long talk with my daughter about using public restrooms, and how she always needed to make a decision before using any of them.

As I explained it to her, "You have two choices: you either hover above the toilet seat, while trying not to touch anything, or you cover it with paper before sitting down. It's either one or the other— hover or cover," I told her.

I also explained that, once she'd made the decision to hover, there was no sitting down allowed. Then I told her to please never, ever push Mommy down while she was trying to hover again.

ONE SICK KID

Our son, who was around two years old at the time, was very sick one day. He was relaxing on the couch when I suddenly started to hear that noise we all knew and dread when he was getting ready to throw up.

I immediately grabbed him and ran toward the nearest sink, away from all rug and fabric-covered surfaces, trying to avoid a massive clean-up.

We'd made it as far as the kitchen and that's when it all let loose, hitting the floor, the wall, the kitchen table and chairs, and all over my poor, sick child, who now looked confused and was probably wondering why any mother would suddenly grab her child and run when all they were trying to do was throw up.

We stood there in the kitchen for a few seconds as I tried to assess the situation. There was barf covering what seemed like every surface imaginable.

I looked down to make sure he was done throwing up. He looked okay, but still confused and frozen in place, not knowing quite what to do.

I then looked down at myself. *I didn't get any on me! Yay!*

Silly me…I should have known that wouldn't be the worst of it.

I yelled to my daughter, who was around seven years old at the time, to please come help, and to bring the wet wipes. Hearing me yell in a somewhat urgent manner, she came running as fast as she could into the kitchen and around the corner, still in her nightclothes and bare feet, wearing nothing but shorts and an old T-shirt. She had no idea why I wanted the wipes, but she was on a mission, and was very eager to help out Mom.

Unfortunately, she didn't see the mess on the floor. As she came running around the corner, she slipped and fell, full body, into it and immediately started to scream. The nasty mess covered her backside, from head to toe, and her hair and clothes were completely soaked in it. I now had two children and an entire kitchen totally covered in barf.

My daughter was still lying in a mess that she didn't know how to get out of without slipping and falling back into it. I was still holding my son in place, trying to keep him from spreading the mess even further.

I didn't know what to do first. *Which child should I tend to first?*

I couldn't help myself—I started laughing hysterically. The kids didn't quite know what to do, and stood frozen in place—giving me some extremely dirty looks.

Why was Mom laughing? This is not funny!

My sides were starting to hurt now. I couldn't stop laughing!

I decided to call my husband at work to tell him what had happened. The kids were still not finding it amusing at this point, but he and his coworkers found it funny as hell.

As I was talking on the phone, I started gathering the wet wipes and tried to figure out where, what, and who to start cleaning first. I then quickly finished my conversation, because they were now starting to move and I didn't want the mess to spread.

I helped my daughter up off the floor and decided to clean her off a bit first. Then I started working on my son.

I'd finally cleaned them enough so they could make it to the shower without leaving a trail on the way to the bathroom.

After they'd both taken showers and had thoroughly washed their hair several times, it was time to clean up the mess in the kitchen.

Hours later, I was still cleaning and still laughing. I don't think I've ever laughed so hard while cleaning up such a nasty mess in my entire life.

Years later, this is still my favorite story. The kids do laugh about it now. I guess these stories are funnier after they've grown up and started to look at it from a parent's point of view, and not of the child who was covered in barf at the time.

ᴄᴷᴼCONCLUSION

So...WHAT DO YOU THINK?

Are we normal?

Does this kind of stuff happen to you, too? Do you know someone who can relate extremely well to one of these stories, or just happens to have one of those funny stories you just can't forget? Everyone has that one hysterical moment in time when they were growing up or something happened to them at work or at home, or one of their kids.

If you have a funny story you'd like to share with the world, we want to hear from you. To have your story included in our upcoming book, *Are We Normal, Part Two*, please visit our website at www.AreWeNormal.com

And if you enjoyed this book, please tell your friends. Leave a review on the website where you purchased it, or send us an email at:

AreWeNormal@yahoo.com

Thank you!

ABOUT THE AUTHOR

Christina Scalise is a wife, mother of three, author, professional organizer, creator, and owner of Organize Your Life and More and OrganizeYourLifeAndMore.com. She is also a certified Reiki master/teacher. She resides in upstate New York with her family and enjoys writing, gardening, outdoor activities, organizing just about anything, and most of all, spending time with her friends and family.

Other books written by Christina Scalise:

Organize Your Finances, Your Kids, Your Life!

Organize Your Life and More

CPSIA information can be obtained
at www.ICGtesting.com
Printed in the USA
LVHW010425010322
712230LV00006B/279